SHAKESPEARE'S DRAMATIC CHALLENGE

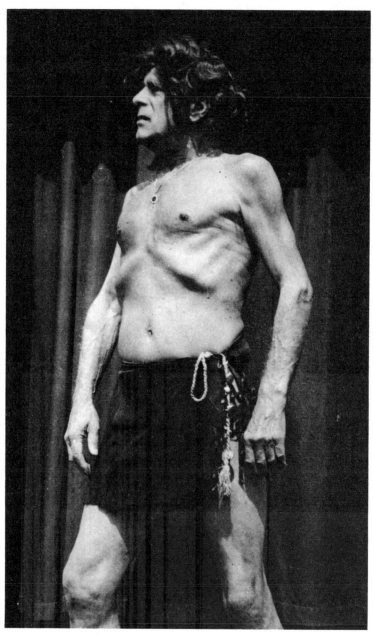

Wilson Knight as Timon (1976)

Photograph by Hilary Clarke

SHAKESPEARE'S DRAMATIC CHALLENGE

ON THE RISE OF SHAKESPEARE'S
TRAGIC HEROES

G. WILSON KNIGHT

In Death I see not overthrow — Ibsen, *Brand*

CROOM HELM   LONDON

BARNES & NOBLE BOOKS · NEW YORK
(a division of Harper & Row Publishers, Inc.)

© 1977 G. Wilson Knight

Croom Helm Ltd.,
2-10 St John's Road, London SW11

ISBN 0-85664-309-2

Reprinted 1977

Published in the U.S.A. 1977 by
HARPER & ROW PUBLISHERS, INC.
BARNES & NOBLE IMPORT DIVISION
ISBN 0-06-493823-9
LC 76-40875

Printed and bound in Great Britain by
Redwood Burn Limited, Trowbridge & Esher

CONTENTS

By the same author

The Wheel of Fire (Tragedies)
The Imperial Theme (Tragedies)
The Crown of Life (Final Plays)
The Shakespearian Tempest (Symbolism)
The Sovereign Flower (Royalism; General Index)
The Mutual Flame (Sonnets and 'The Phoenix and the Turtle')
Shakespearian Production
Shakespeare and Religion
Vergil and Shakespeare (Memorial Lecture)

On Other Poets

Poets of Action (Spenser, Milton, Swift, Byron)
The Starlit Dome (Wordsworth, Coleridge, Shelley, Keats)
Laureate of Peace; reissued as *The Poetry of Pope*
Lord Byron: Christian Virtues
Lord Byron's Marriage
Byron and Shakespeare
The Golden Labyrinth (on British drama)
Ibsen
The Saturnian Quest (John Cowper Powys)
Neglected Powers (Modern Literature)

On Poetry and Religion

The Christian Renaissance (The New Testament, Dante, Goethe)
Christ and Nietzsche (Christian Dogma, Germanic Philosophy and
Thus Spake Zarathustra)
Hiroshima (Literature and the Atomic Bomb)

General

Atlantic Crossing
The Dynasty of Stowe

Drama

The Last of the Incas

Biography

Jackson Knight: a Biography

Poetry

Gold-Dust

Tape Recordings (USA)

Shakespeare's Rhetoric
Shakespeare and the English Language
Byron's Rhetoric

Video-Tape

Shakespeare's Dramatic Challenge (page 152)

ACKNOWLEDGEMENTS

Gratitude must be expressed, for my use of quotations, to the following:

John Baker (Publishers) Ltd and the Estate of the late C.B. Purdom
  (What Happens in Shakespeare)
Flammarion et Cie
  (Reflections on the Theatre by Jean-Louis Barrault, translated by
    Barbara Wall)
Faber and Faber Ltd, Alfred A. Knopf, Inc. and Dr George Steiner
  (The Death of Tragedy)
Faber and Faber Ltd, Harcourt Brace Jovanovich and Mrs Valerie Eliot
  (T.S. Eliot's *Selected Essays,* 'Seneca and Elizabethan Translation')
Macdonald and Jane's Publishers Ltd and the Estate of John Cowper
Powys
  (Rodmoor)
Macmillan, London and Basingstoke and the Estate of the late
A.C. Bradley
  (Shakespearean Tragedy)
Gollancz (Victor) Ltd
  (Bernard Shaw and Mrs Patrick Campbell: their correspondence,
    ed. Alan Dent)
The Oxford University Press and Mr Glen Cavaliero
  (John Cowper Powys, Novelist)
The University of North Carolina Press and Dr Thomas Macfarland
  (Shakespeare's Pastoral Comedy)
Maurice Barbanell, editor of *Two Worlds*
  (The Essene Gospel of John)
George Allen & Unwin (Publishers) Ltd
  (Indian Philosophy by Radakrishnan)

FOR OLIVIA MORDUE ANDERSON
whose support of my recital has
given me encouragement and strength

PREFACE

I record my gratitude to the *Times Literary Supplement,* which first printed the essay on Granville-Barker used in my Appendix; to Professor Henri Suhamy, for my use of his valuable paragraph on *Julius Caesar;* and to Mr Roy Walker for giving me permission to quote from a private letter which he addressed to me after seeing my Leeds *Timon of Athens* (page 174). I am indebted to the Editor of the *Exeter University Club Bulletin* and to Mrs Andrew Anderson (Miss Olivia Mordue) for my use of a generous review which gives a valuable impression of my recital (page 153).

For secretarial help I am indebted to Mrs Gordon Lothian, Miss Pamela Ffooks, Mrs C.E. Newson and Mrs Caroline Belgrave; and, as always, I am grateful to Mr John D. Christie for his expert care in reading my proofs and making my index. Miss Judith Bennett has been active in seeing my book through the press. I thank Mrs Amy Swannell for aid with my recital costumes. Both the City and University Libraries at Exeter have provided continual assistance.

The video-tape now being done at Yeovil (page 152) will give a faithful report of the recital. The letters of Powys to myself, relevant to this book, are being published as *Powys to Knight,* edited by Professor Robert Blackmore (Cecil Woolf). I was recently much impressed by the visual body-effects of Mr Christopher Plummer's performance in the 1969 film version of *The Royal Hunt of the Sun,* as shown on television.

My line references apply to the Oxford Shakespeare.

At Wyoming the internationally renowned sculptor, Robert I. Russin, after witnessing my recital, suggested doing a Head to record its dramatic effect; and more recently, in Devonshire, Kenneth Carter, creator of the sculptures in the Chapter House of Exeter Cathedral, has made a full-length study. I am honoured by the attention given to me by such artists.

One last word: it is important to realise that my dramatic recital lies behind my whole book, however 'academic' some of the discussions may appear.

Exeter, Summer 1976   G.W.K.

FOREWORD

Since this book has grown from my dramatic recital 'Shakespeare's Dramatic Challenge', a prefatory note on my stage experience will be helpful. The complete record, with illustrations, has already been documented in *Shakespearian Production* (enlarged 1964), but a rather more personal account is offered here.

After leaving Oxford in 1923 I started writing on Shakespeare; but long before that, since I was a boy at Dulwich, I had been an ardent follower of Shakespearian productions in London, and in particular those of Beerbohm Tree and Granville-Barker: I have written of them in *Shakespearian Production*. I did not get an opportunity to act myself until I went to Cheltenham to teach at Dean Close School in 1925. During my years there, I acted in productions by the British Empire Shakespeare Society and produced plays at the School. I followed W. Bridges-Adams' Stratford productions with avidity.

After going to the University of Toronto my stage work was extended. I was able to put on my own productions at Hart House Theatre (in the University grounds but not at that time part of the University), and, having complete control, I gained the experience of playing leading parts: Romeo, Hamlet, Othello, Lear, Timon, Leontes and Caliban. There was also the Shakespeare Society of Toronto; for this Society I produced, and acted. After a while, the Society combined with my own productions. I also played in Brownlow Card's productions, doing Brutus and Macbeth. Toronto was during those years a vital centre of dramatic interest and ability; under amateur conditions, but enjoying the participation of ex-professionals and amateurs as good as any professional. One summer I played Hamlet a second time at the Rudolf Steiner Hall, London.

My academic writing was simultaneously active. This might appear to stand apart from my stage work, but such a judgement would be superficial. My commentaries have always been characterised by exploitation of what Nietzsche calls the 'Dionysian' element in drama; far more so, by the way, than were Granville-Barker's *Prefaces*. I made some attempt to define the relation of these two, stage and academic, sides to my work in *Principles of Shakespearian Production* in 1936. I also developed a technique of dramatic recital.

These recitals were sometimes about Shakespeare's kings, and
when the war came in 1939, they took a national form. This was the
easier, since I had published an article on *Henry VIII*, and produced it
for the Shakespeare Society of Toronto. Being strongly convinced
of Shakespeare's responsibility for the work, and especially for
Cranmer's national prophecy at the conclusion, I was enabled to
view Shakespeare's national statement as follows: (i) simple patriotism,
leading to *Henry V;* (ii) a plunge into the deeps of the great tragedies,
with their nihilistic revulsions and war-satire, culminating in *Timon of
Athens;* and (iii) an emergence into the purified nationalism of
Cranmer's prophecy.

This gradually became fixed as a powerful recital and after I had left
Toronto and returned to England in the spring of 1940, I gave it at
various centres; first in collaboration with Nancy Price and afterwards
alone, working up to my week at the Westminster Theatre, London,
in the summer of 1941. Earlier recitals had been a mixture of lecture,
reading and acting, in ordinary clothes; but for the Westminster Theatre
more was needed, and I used costume changes and effects, especially
for the great tragedies, where I had the support of Henry Ainley,
coming from retirement to read my written commentaries while I was
preparing to go on. My main production emphasis was on *Timon of
Athens;* in part because I had recently done it at Toronto and was
personally involved in it, and in part because its relevance, and in
particular its comment on 'contumelious, beastly, mad-brain'd war',
was so keen. I was the only actor, though I had tried to enlist
collaborators; but, as so often in my life, I was thrown back on myself,
and my lonely vision. The Ministry of Information, though approached
again and again, showed no interest; with a small team it might have
toured the United States to considerable effect, as it was not then in
the war. An account of *This Sceptred Isle,* with *The Times'* review of
it, appears in my *Shakespearian Production* (1964). The late
C.B. Purdom, biographer of Granville-Barker, wrote to me: 'You
attempted a task such as not even the greatest actors have tried, and
you succeeded through sheer intellectual force and physical courage.'

My interest in *Timon of Athens* was not independent of the element
of nudity required by the performance. Stage nudity was already a
concern of mine, and I had practised in semi-nude parts. Timon was
a culmination. I added an essay 'The Body Histrionic' on the importance
of stage nudity (composed in 1939) to my *Principles of Shakespearian
Production* (Penguin edition, 1948). Since then, nudity has become a

widespread stage practice, sometimes powerful, sometimes pointless.

At Leeds I had opportunities for more full-length performances: Timon, Lear, Othello and Shylock (which was new to me). All but Timon were produced by others: by, respectively, John Boorman, Arthur Creedy, Frederick May. For these opportunities with either the Leeds University Union Theatre Group, of which I was President, or the Staff Dramatic Society, I remain deeply grateful.

In 1964 I published *Shakespearian Production,* a much amplified version of my earlier book.

Lecturing was, naturally, a major occupation, either at the University of Leeds or elsewhere. Often these lectures were nearer to recitals than lectures; and after my retirement in 1962, straight acting being now outside my life-pattern, my recitals became more and more acted performances. A certain transfixing quality is attained by such acted recitals which neither a full-length performance nor a formal lecture by themselves possess; the audience gets moments of living drama *together with meaning,* a new dimension being added to their engagement and receptivity. I gave performances sometimes on the way that Shakespeare's long speeches build up and flower (see page 49 below); and another, on the rising quality of Shakespeare's tragedies and tragic heroes. This latter I gave to the Devonshire Association, Dulwich College, and elsewhere in 1971, and it soon began to have a peculiarly sharp and effective focus that gripped my audiences. Intimation of this was particularly clear at Eton College and at St David's College, Lampeter, both in 1973. I also gave it at the West Country Writers' Association at Exeter in 1973; and at other centres, including the World Centre for Shakespeare Studies (Bankside Globe Association, London); the Shakespeare Institute of Stratford-upon-Avon; and university literary societies at the Royal Holloway College and at Exeter, Aberystwyth, Birmingham and Newcastle; and at Blundell's School. I took it to eight Canadian universities (at Ottawa, Regina, Guelph, Hamilton, Toronto, Montreal, Halifax and St John's) in a tour organised by Professor Alistair Tilson, of Carleton University, Ottawa, in 1974; and in 1975 to ten universities in the Rocky Mountain area of the United States (in Los Angeles, Arizona, New Mexico, Colorado and Wyoming), the tour organised by Professor Walter Edens of the University of Wyoming, and under the daily control of Mr Fred Cannan, who looked after all details, driving from place to place and arranging motels. The tour was supplemented by visits to four more universities in Texas (at Austin,

College Station, San Marcos and Waco), organised by Professor Walter Eggers of Wyoming and Professor John Welz of the University of Texas. I was accompanied throughout my American travels by Miss Olivia Mordue (now Mrs Andrew Anderson). To all those, in Canada and the United States, and indeed in England and Wales too, who have helped me, and to the many audiences for their generous reception, I record my heart-felt gratitude. Then came the kind Northcott Theatre invitation from Mr Geoffrey Reeves, and the recital expanded. About this expansion, I say more in Part II, below. Three performances were given at the International Shakespeare Association Congress at Washington, in April 1976; and some repeat performances are to be given at the Northcott Theatre in the coming autumn.

PART 1: THE HEROES DISCUSSED

1 INTRODUCTION

My purpose is to set down on paper the substance of a lecture-recital that I have been giving widely for some years, on the way Shakespeare's dark tragedies, culminating in *Timon of Athens,* celebrate a poetic rise rather than any fall. This recital has been in process of development for a long time; some of it is already written into my book *Shakespearian Production,* but its effect there remains blunted, if only because of the other material contained. In my lectures, or recitals, it has become sharper as the years go by, and has now reached, as I see it, its final shape. So I set it down in writing, in an expanded form.

Since I am to be involved with the poetry and its extension into dramatic action, it may be as well to point retrospectively to my Prefatory Note to the 1947 reissue of *The Wheel of Fire,* where I wrote:

> But my experience as actor, producer and play-goer leaves me uncompromising in my assertion that the literary analysis of great drama in terms of theatrical technique accomplishes singularly little. Such technicalities should be confined to the theatre from which their terms are drawn.

True, I had already before that gone some way to breaking the barrier in my *Principles of Shakespearian Production,* and was to go much further in the much enlarged reissue of the book entitled *Shakespearian Production* in 1964. My *Wheel of Fire* statement was, in its way, an admission of defeat, though a defeat in a matter where no victory has, at least to my knowledge, ever been recorded. What is involved is the discrepancy between Shakespeare's supposed persons and the poetry which they speak. Twice in Shakespeare this problem is highlighted. In *Julius Caesar* Antony says:

> I am no orator as Brutus is,
> But as you know me all, a plain blunt man.
>
> (III.ii.221)

And yet he makes a famous oration. We have to make allowances for — what? The character's deception? Shakespeare's artistry? It is not easy, and even more confusing is Othello's denial of his own superb poetry:

> Rude am I in my speech
> And little bless'd with the soft phrase of peace;
> For since these arms of mine had seven years' pith,
> Till now some nine moons wasted, they have us'd
> Their dearest action in the tented field; . . .

(I.iii.81)

We may say that he is in this speech expressing the quality of blunt soldiership in an adequate poetry; but this scarcely covers elsewhere what I have called his peculiar 'music'. With Macbeth it is regularly in dispute as to how much of his superb imaginative apprehension is to be attributed to himself and how much to Shakespeare's artistry. It is an extraordinarily difficult problem. In this book I do no more than throw out a few suggestions. The field is new, and complete success is not to be expected.

I shall now concentrate on the poetry of Shakespeare's tragic heroes; not, for my immediate purpose, Shakespeare's tragedies as wholes, so much as on the heroes; and especially the heroes' poetry at the play's conclusions. I have often written and lectured on Shakespeare's long speeches, on the way they accumulate power, and rise; or start on an ordinary level and later disclose some imagistic or poetic gem or symbol that interprets and justifies the whole. Now it is the same with the hero's story in the tragedies: it rises, and rises, above all, poetically. In the need for a proper realisation of this poetic and dramatic 'rise' exists what I call Shakespeare's 'dramatic challenge'.

2 EARLY TRAGEDY

Titus Andronicus (?1592-4) has only of late come into critical
perspective. We may regard it a precursor of *King Lear* as a study of
suffering age. Titus refuses imperial responsibility and hands over
power to Saturninus; not unlike Lear giving over his kingship to his
daughters. He is, like Lear, irascible. He is guilty of the callous sacrifice
of a prisoner of war. Tamora, the conquered Gothic queen, pleads for
her son's life:

> Gracious conqueror,
> Victorious Titus, rue the tears I shed,
> A mother's tears in passion for her son.

(I.i.104)

Titus is adamant. The comment of a Goth is: 'Was ever Scythia half so
barbarous?' (I.i.131). After that, as though by a kind of retribution,
he is impelled to kill his own son, as Lear rejects Cordelia in anger.

What follows is swift and terrible. Tamora marries the new emperor
Saturninus and acts in collusion with her lover, the evil Moor, Aaron.
The Goths gain influence and power. Titus soon finds himself among
'a wilderness of tigers' (III.i.54).* Rome's ingratitude to one who had
so often proved her saviour in war (pages 119-20 below) is horribly
evident. As troubles crowd on him, Titus gains poetic stature:

> If there were reason for these miseries
> Then into limits could I bend my woes.
> When heaven doth weep, doth not the earth o'erflow?
> If the winds rage, doth not the sea wax mad,
> Threatening the welkin with his big-swoln face?
> And wilt thou have a reason for this coil?
> I am the sea; hark, how her sighs do blow.
> She is the weeping welkin, I the earth. . .

(III.i.219)

*The quotation gives the title to a remarkable essay on *Titus Andronicus* by
Alan Sommers: 'Wilderness of Tigers', *Essays in Criticism,* July 1960, X.3.

Somewhat laboured, but the accents of tragic poetry are there. Titus gains a strange insight through his sufferings:

> *Titus.* What doth thou strike at, Marcus, with thy knife?
> *Marcus.* At·that that I have kill'd, my lord − a fly.
> *Titus.* Out on thee, murderer! Thou kill'st my heart.
> Mine eyes are cloy'd with view of tyranny.
> A deed of death done on the innocent
> Becomes not Titus' brother: get thee gone.
> I see thou art not for my company.
> *Marcus.* Alas, my lord, I have but kill'd a fly.
> *Titus.* But how if that fly had a father and a mother?
> How would he hang his slender gilded wings
> And buzz lamenting doings in the air.
> Poor harmless fly,
> That with his pretty buzzing melody
> Came here to make us merry! And thou hast kill'd him.

(III.ii.52)

He has travelled far since his early ruthless actions. It is this advance on Titus' part that saves the story from being no more than an accumulation of horrors.

I say the 'story', but the poetry is another matter. It swells and subsides with considerable power. Titus sometimes pretends to be mad, like Hamlet, or perhaps he is mad, like Lear, or half-mad; distraught by the calamities that have fallen on him. The rampaging villainies include the raping of his daughter Lavinia by Tamora's two iniquitous sons, and their cutting off of her hands and tongue. Titus' own hand is, by a trick, subsequently cut off also, and two of his other sons killed. Within this barbarous and criminal community Titus cries out not merely for revenge but for justice. He sends, or thinks that he sends, a messenger to the Underworld, but Pluto replies that, though he can help with Revenge, justice is to be found in Heaven; so Titus arranges that his friends shoot arrows with missives addressed to the various gods. This fantastically conceived extravaganza serves, in a manner characteristic of Shakespearian tragedy, to give the middle-action new life and impetus. It lifts us beyond revenge and we regard the final horrors as actions of justice. Titus is busily purposeful and his plot matures with strength and efficiency. He kills Tamora's two sons, and serves them up to her at a banquet. He has

gone from strength to strength. Though the play's substances are
horrible, the emotional and poetic correspondents are handled in
masterly fashion and the artistry is on occasion superb.

We have here as deep a study of evil as could well be offered
without reliance on supernatural categories. Evil is in part caused by
circumstances, in part ingrained. Titus' early actions call down his
later sufferings. The Goths have reason for hating and disrupting Rome.
The Moor, Aaron, our main agent of wickedness, is a solitary figure,
who may be supposed to have suffered from racial antipathy. He is
black. The nurse calls his son by Tamora a 'devil', because black
(IV.ii.65). Tamora's sons would have it killed, to preserve her honour,
but he replies in accents of courage (and imagery pointing ahead to
Othello; see page 32 below) that arouse our admiration:

> Now by the burning tapers of the sky,
> That shone so brightly when this boy was got,
> He dies upon my scimitar's sharp point
> That touches this my first-born son and heir.

(IV.ii.90)

He would dare 'great Alcides' in this cause:

> What, what, ye sanguine, shallow-hearted boys!
> Ye white-lim'd walls, ye alehouse painted signs!
> Coal-black is better than another hue,
> In that it scorns to bear another hue.

(IV.ii.98)

His appearance and pride forecast Morocco in *The Merchant of Venice,*
and also perhaps Othello, though his part here is that of an Iago. He is
almost ludicrously proud of his wicked actions. His evil nature is so
ingrained that it wins a kind of respect, as does Iago's; and both look
to death in torment with equanimity. This approach to evil has an
indirect bearing on Shakespeare's later treatment of Richard III and
Macbeth.

The evil in Aaron is so extreme that it raises metaphysical questions
regarding the authority of evil in the universe. The dastardly raping and
mutilation of Lavinia were performed in what seems an evil part of
the forest. Its horror was elaborately described (II.iii.90-108). Later
Titus remembers it, while turning over the pages of Ovid's

Metamorphoses:

> *Titus.* Lavinia, wert thou thus surpris'd, sweet girl,
> Ravish'd and wrong'd, as Philomela was,
> Forc'd in the ruthless, vast, and gloomy woods?
> See, see!
> Ay, such a place there is, where we did hunt —
> O! Had we never, never hunted there —
> Pattern'd by that the poet here describes,
> By nature made for murders and for rapes.
> *Marcus.* O, why should nature build so foul a den,
> Unless the gods delight in tragedies?

(IV.i.51)

Is there even a questioning here regarding the cruelty of blood-sports? For the rest, nature, apart from tempests and fierce beasts, is usually idyllic in Shakespeare. Can it be that Providence and Nature are, in some moods, malignant? And that human evil has authority behind it?

I pass over *King John* (?1590-6), which is not strictly a study of a tragic hero at all. It is in the main a political drama, forecasting the pattern of *Cymbeline.* The king ends with a happy outcome to his problems, making peace with the Church of Rome, though he himself dies from a poison, suffering rather like Marlowe's Tamburlaine. The emphasis throughout is political, or national, with the bastard Falconbridge as England's voice.

In *Richard III* (about 1593) we have a wicked protagonist. His opening soliloquy gives us a psychological analysis of his motives, but during the early scenes he becomes an extravagant conception, almost a comic buffoon, like Marlowe's Jew in *The Jew of Malta.* With Buckingham's help, he attains the throne, and when he first enters as king, a new dignity is apparent. Buckingham has been his accomplice and supporter hitherto, and Richard now hints that he would like the princes in the Tower murdered. Buckingham's response is no more than tentative and arouses Richard's comment: 'High reaching Buckingham grows circumspect' (IV.ii.31). Buckingham claims the earldom promised him for his long service, but Richard is withdrawn, and meditative, with a certain foreboding. He thinks of a prophecy that Richmond should be King:

> *Buckingham.* My lord, your promise for the earldom —
> *King Richard.* Richmond. When last I was at Exeter
> The Mayor in courtesy show'd me the castle,
> And call'd it 'Rougemont': at which name I started,
> Because a bard of Ireland told me once
> I should not live long after I saw Richmond.
> *Buckingham.* My lord!
> *King Richard.* Ay, what's o'clock?
> *Buckingham.* I am thus bold to put your Grace in mind
> Of what you promis'd me.
> *King Richard.* Well, but what is't o'clock?
> *Buckingham.*   Upon the stroke of ten.
> *King Richard.* Well, let it strike.
> *Buckingham.*   Why let it strike?
> *King Richard.* Because that, like a Jack, thou keep'st the stroke
> Betwixt thy begging and my meditation.
> I am not in the giving vein to-day.
> *Buckingham.* Why, then, resolve me whether you will, or no.
> *King Richard.* Thou troublest me: I am not in the vein.
>
> (IV.ii.101)

Richard is our protagonist; he now enjoys the additional pomp and insignia of regality, probably wearing a great robe.* We see him in a new light, and though he is himself overpoweringly guilty, we thoroughly enjoy watching him disappoint the hopes of his companion in crime. He has become an agent of judgement. The scene acts as a pivot. Richard has now a new dignity and the play enjoys an access of power.

Before the Battle of Bosworth his accents are those of tragic dignity, and should so be spoken, with, again, foreboding:

> Up with my tent. Here will I lie tonight;
> But where to-morrow? Well, all's one for that.
>
> (V.iii.7)

---

*I am thinking of Sir Donald Wolfit in this scene, where he made the crimson robe flash out with extraordinary effect at the climax, as a tongue of fire. Wolfit was an adept in making robes speak.

And:

>   I will not sup to-night.
>   Give me some ink and paper.
>   What, is my beaver easier than it was?

(V.iii.48)

These touches come disjointedly, among other thoughts. We are
personally attuned to Richard's personal burdens:

>   Saddle white Surrey for the field to-morrow.
>   Look that my staves be sound, and not too heavy.

(V.iii.64)

These impressions are summed in:

>   Give me a bowl of wine.
>   I have not that alacrity of spirit,
>   Nor cheer of mind, that I was wont to have.

(V.iii.72)

'Alacrity': a wonderful word, characteristic — I do not know why — of
Richard. We no longer watch Richard objectively; we are, at such
moments, within his personal experience.

After he has been visited in sleep by the ghosts of his victims, his
soliloquy builds up, in the usual style of Shakespeare's long speeches,
from a beginning in ambivalence and psychological confusion, playing
on the enigma of conscience, to a firm statement of self-condemnation:

>   *King Richard* (waking). Give me another horse! Bind up my
>   wounds!
>   Have mercy, Jesu! Soft — I did but dream.
>   O coward conscience, how dost thou afflict me!
>   The lights burn blue. It is now dead midnight.
>   Cold fearful drops stand on my trembling flesh.
>   What do I fear? Myself? There's none else by.
>   Richard loves Richard: that is, I am I.
>   Is there a murderer here? No. Yes, I am.
>   Then fly: what! from myself? Great reason why:
>   Lest I revenge. What, myself upon myself?

Alack, I love myself. Wherefore? For any good
That I myself have done unto myself?
O, no, alas! I rather hate myself
For hateful deeds committed by myself.
I am a villain. Yet I lie; I am not.
Fool, of thyself speak well. Fool, do not flatter.
My conscience hath a thousand several tongues,
And every tongue brings in a several tale,
And every tale condemns me for a villain.
Perjury, perjury, in the high'st degree;
Murder, stern murder in the dir'st degree;
All several sins, all us'd in each degree,
Throng to the bar, crying all, 'Guilty, guilty!'
I shall despair. There is no creature loves me,
And if I die, no soul will pity me.
Nay, wherefore should they, since that I myself
Find in myself no pity to myself?
Methought the souls of all that I had murder'd
Came to my tent, and every one did threat
Tomorrow's vengeance on the head of Richard.

(V.iii.178)

A remarkable speech in its play on the antagonism, within an
individual, of evil and conscience. Richard finally accepts the
reality of his guilt; without repentance but also without self-pity.
The speech casts light, differently, on the King in *Hamlet,* and
Macbeth. Richard is disturbed:

   King Richard.   O Ratcliff, I fear, I fear —
   Ratcliff. Nay, good my lord, be not afraid of shadows.
   King Richard. By the apostle Paul, shadows tonight
Have struck more terror to the soul of Richard
Than can the substance of ten thousand soldiers,
Armèd in proof and led by shallow Richmond.

(V.iii.215)

Despite his villainies, Richard swears regularly by St Paul (I.i.138;
I.ii.36,41; I.iii.45; III.iv.75), who seems to have been an especial
favourite, perhaps because of a tradition that he was, like Richard,
deformed. 'Soul', an important word in Shakespeare, is used for

Richard's higher self and the seat of conscience. Though fear-struck
by 'shadows', he is opposed only by a 'shallow' enemy. The word
is significant: whatever his sins, Richard has the status of a tragic
hero, studied in depth.

Countering Richard's wickedness — or because of it? — we feel a
certain sympathy, and even approval. There is no final paradox.
Richard's valuations, in descent from Aaron's in *Titus Andronicus,*
are consistent:

> Conscience is but a word that cowards use
> Devis'd at first to keep the strong in awe.
> Our strong arms be our conscience, swords our law.
> March on, join bravely, let us to't pell-mell,
> If not to Heaven, then hand in hand to Hell.

> (V.iii.310)

Courage is aligned with wickedness, but it is still courage and has
nobility. So has his patriotism: Richard's address to his army is quite
remarkable. Shakespeare's worst king-villain not only conquers his
fears, but becomes the voice for one of Shakespeare's most fervent
speeches of national defiance:

> Let's whip these stragglers o'er the sea again;
> Lash hence these overweening rags of France,
> These famish'd beggars, weary of their lives;
> Who, but for dreaming on this fond exploit,
> For want of means, poor rats, had hang'd themselves.
> If we be conquer'd, let men conquer us,
> And not these bastard Bretons; whom our fathers
> Have in their own land beaten, bobb'd, and thump'd
> And, on record, left them the heirs of shame.
> Shall these enjoy our lands? Lie with our wives?
> Ravish our daughters? Hark! I hear their drum.
> Fight, gentlemen of England! Fight, bold yeomen!
> Draw, archers, draw your arrows to the head!
> Spur your proud horses hard, and ride in blood;
> Amaze the welkin with your broken staves!

> (V.iii.328)

All Shakespeare's impassioned patriotism is here; and the speech is given to wicked Richard.

To the last he is brave. The ghosts may have shown him a deeper truth, but this 'truth' he masters, even, we may say, transcends. Like Talbot in *1 Henry VI* (II.iii.50-63), he feels himself a multitudinous Titanic power:

> A thousand hearts are great within my bosom.
> Advance our standards! Set upon our foes!
> Our ancient word of courage, fair Saint George,
> Inspire us with the spleen of fiery dragons!
> Upon them! Victory sits upon our helms.
>
> (V.iii.348)

Notice how Shakespeare's usual patriotic battle-cry is cleverly aligned with its opposite, so that Richard stands not merely for Saint George as against the Dragon, but for Saint George *and* the Dragon; as though he were in a state beyond good and evil. According to Nietzsche, the transcending of the good-and-evil opposition touches superhumanity. So Richard is a super-hero:

> The King enacts more wonders than a man,
> Daring an opposite to every danger:
> His horse is slain, and all on foot he fights,
> Seeking for Richmond in the throat of death.
>
> (V.iv.2)

He himself is, like Macbeth, finally uncertain yet unbending:

> I have set my life upon a cast,
> And I will stand the hazard of the die.
> I think there be six Richmonds in the field;
> Five have I slain to-day, instead of him. —
> A horse! a horse! My kingdom for a horse!
>
> (V.iv.9)

He meets Richmond, and is slain, but not until he has left in our minds an indelible impression of tragic heroism.

So *Richard III* ends well. *Richard II* (1595-6) is equally, or more, impressive. Richard is at the start unsure of himself, and is shown in the early scenes irresponsible and repellent. On his return from his Irish expedition he speaks finely of England's earth and the innate

power of kingship to resist insurrection. The poetry has splendour.
When the Sun is hidden crimes abound:

> But when, from under this terrestrial ball
> He fires the proud tops of the eastern pines
> And darts his light through every guilty hole,
> Then murders, treasons, and detested sins,
> The cloak of night being pluck'd from off their backs,
> Stand bare and naked, trembling at themselves.
> So when this thief, this traitor, Bolingbroke,
> Who all this while hath revell'd in the night
> Whilst we were wandering with the antipodes,
> Shall see us rising in our throne, the east,
> His treasons will sit blushing in his face,
> Not able to endure the sight of day,
> But self-affrighted tremble at his sin.
> Not all the water in the rough rude sea
> Can wash the balm from an anointed king;
> The breath of worldly men cannot depose
> The deputy elected by the Lord.

(III.ii.41)

For every rebel that opposes him, God sends a 'glorious angel' to fight on
his side. Richard's 'character' need not be supposed to have changed,
but it is overshadowed by his royalty, whose language is poetry.
George Steiner has well remarked that Richard 'is a royal poet defeated
by a rebellion of prose' *(The Death of Tragedy , 1961, p.242)*. The
play is dominated by the poetry of royalty.

But bad news follows. Richard becomes quickly humble, abased,
in despair almost; religious thoughts come in to give what comfort
they may. He thinks of death, and the murders of past kings, and the
absurdity of ceremonial reverence for one who is no more than a
simple man. Then, encouraged by a supporter, he becomes again
confident of success. There is more bad news, and he despairs.

Before Flint Castle, he addresses Northumberland. Again he is a
king, and speaks with authority; with now an *added* authority, partly
because the speech takes in the imponderables of futurity:

> We are amaz'd; and thus long have we stood
> To watch the fearful bending of thy knee,

Because we thought ourself thy lawful king:
And if we be, how dare thy joints forget
To pay their awful duty to our presence?
If we be not, show us the hand of God
That hath dismiss'd us from our stewardship;
For well we know, no hand of blood and bone
Can gripe the sacred handle of our sceptre,
Unless he do profane, steal or usurp.
And though you think that all, as you have done,
Have torn their souls by turning them from us,
And we are barren and bereft of friends;
Yet know, my master, God omnipotent,
Is mustering in his clouds on our behalf
Armies of pestilence; and they shall strike
Your children yet unborn and unbegot,
That lift your vassal hands against my head
And threat the glory of my precious crown.
Tell Bolingbroke — for yond methinks he is —
That every stride he makes upon my land
Is dangerous treason: he is come to open
The purple testament of bleeding war;
But ere the crown he looks for live in peace,
Ten thousand bloody crowns of mothers' sons
Shall ill become the flower of England's face,
Change the complexion of her maid-pale peace
To scarlet indignation, and bedew
Her pastures' grass with faithful English blood.

                                                    (III.iii.72)

This is Richard's best speech, so far. It has a rising strength and
assurance, based on royalty. I remember how Maurice Evans electrified
his audience with it in his highly successful New York (though I saw it
in Canada) production, in the nineteen-thirties.

He suffers a reaction:

                    O! that I were as great
As is my grief, or lesser than my name,
Or that I could forget what I have been,
Or not remember what I must be now.

                                                    (III.iii.136)

That is, very precisely, his problem; the discrepancy between himself
as a man, and the greatness of his office. His play shows him trying
to adjust himself to the greatness of his royal poetry; or failing that,
he falls back on religious absolutes. If he 'must lose the name of
King', then 'let it go':

> I'll give my jewels for a set of beads,
> My gorgeous palace for a hermitage,
> My gay apparel for an almsman's gown,
> My figur'd goblets for a dish of wood,
> My sceptre for a palmer's walking-staff,
> My subjects for a pair of carved saints,
> And my large kingdom for a little grave,
> A little little grave, an obscure grave;
> Or I'll be buried in the king's highway,
> Some way of common trade, where subjects' feet
> May hourly trample on their sovereign's head;
> For on my heart they tread now whilst I live.

(III.iii.147)

Like Timon, only less purposefully, he swerves from glory to its
reverse, to a luxury of religious inwardness and resignation.

They go to London. In the Deposition scene Richard first compares
himself to Christ, betrayed by Judas, thereby expressing a fusion of
the two forces, royal and religious, that are now tugging at him; but
he continues humbly enough, relinquishing his crown, and other
insignia, willingly. There seems no more to do, but Northumberland
advances with a paper listing Richard's misdeeds, telling him to read it
aloud, as a witness to the justice of his deposition. Whenever in
Shakespeare a tragic hero appears abased or disintegrated, look for
some grand reassertion. Now, at the moment of apparent degradation,
Richard replies with all the suppressed power that he has been
withholding. The strain has been great, and he now breaks out in
flaming, scorching phrases:

> Must I do so? and must I ravel out
> My weav'd-up follies? Gentle Northumberland,
> If thy offences were upon record,
> Would it not shame thee in so fair a troop
> To read a lecture of them? If thou wouldst

> There shouldst thou find one heinous article,
> Containing the deposing of a king,
> And cracking the strong warrant of an oath,
> Mark'd with a blot, damn'd in the book of Heaven!
> Nay, all of you that stand and look upon me,
> Whilst that my wretchedness doth bait myself,
> Though some of you with Pilate wash your hands,
> Showing an outward pity; yet you Pilates
> Have here deliver'd me to my sour cross,
> And water cannot wash away your sin.

(IV.i.228)

He sees the surrounding company as 'traitors', and includes himself in that category, by reason of his renunciation, having 'made glory base and sovereignty a slave'. His stature is greater than ever. In production, those he addresses should appear not merely embarrassed, but withered, by his cauterising rhetoric.

Naturally, this poetic force cannot be maintained. He falls back on meditative melancholy:

> Say that again.
> The shadow of my sorrow! Ha! let's see:
> 'Tis very true, my grief lies all within;
> And these external manners of laments
> Are merely shadows to the unseen grief
> That swells with silence in the tortur'd soul.

(IV.i.293)

There is a depth in that that may be used widely in our understanding of poetry: however great, it is no more than a provisional expression of the soul-reality behind, or within.

Richard parts with his wife, who urges him to behave less humbly:

> The lion dying thrusteth forth his paw
> And wounds the earth, if nothing else, with rage
> To be o'erpower'd.

(V.i.29)

Humility ill becomes one who is properly 'a lion and a king of beasts'. She is partly wrong. His humility is a recognition of the inevitable, and the lion in him is not crushed.

In the dungeon of Pomfret Castle he speaks a long speech of mystical reverie, packed with interest. He becomes a kind of poet. It is emphasised that the origin of his poetry is the 'soul', in the spiritual order, the earthly brain being subsidiary, though necessary:

> My brain I'll prove the female to my soul;
> My soul the father: and these two beget
> A generation of still-breeding thoughts;
> And these same thoughts people this little world
> In humours like the people of this world,
> For no thought is contented.
>
> (V.v.6)

He is like a dramatic poet, and proceeds, as I have elsewhere (*The Imperial Theme*, XI, 'A note on *Richard II*', p.351) shown, to a series of impressions based on his own experiences and yet also touching Shakespeare's later tragedies, and the fortunes of mankind in general. His review of the human plight is impersonal and objective, as though he were jerked into a state of being above and beyond himself, dispassionately surveying the past and concluding, like Timon:

> Nor I nor any man that but man is
> With nothing shall be pleas'd, till he be eas'd
> With being nothing.
>
> (V.v.39)

In that there is a mysticism, as ambivalent as the Buddhist 'Nirvana', since we can take it that he *is* pleased with not-being; and yet who exists to be pleased? The paradox exists again, even more forcibly, in *Timon of Athens* (see page 138 below). Meanwhile we can say that Richard has touched a mystic truth, and so at this point he hears music. It will be allowed to play for a while, till Richard stops it: it is an all-important event in the action. Richard has been attuned to the poetic dimension, and from there has surveyed his past, while simultaneously forecasting Shakespeare-the-poet's future; and we close in music, corresponding to the music so important in Shakespeare's last plays. It might seem, as so much of Richard's poetry does, 'out of character' with what we saw of him at first;

but we are not thinking of that here, but rather of the fire of his kingly
rhetoric and also the religious deepening of his meditations, whereby
his comparisons of himself to Christ are not at all irelevant; and now
the actual embodiment of poetry in Richard-as-poetic-dramatist
culminates in the mystic intimations of music.

The rest of the soliloquy, in which Richard returns to his present
situation, is less important, though necessary. Because he has not
properly measured up 'to the music of men's lives', he grows irritated
and thinks the player faulty: 'This music mads me' (V.v.44,61). Yet,
characteristically — characteristic I mean, of the charity we shall note
in other Shakespearian heroes as they approach their end — he
pronounces a 'blessing on his heart that gives it me' (V.v.64).
In order to make clearer what Shakespeare is doing we can point to
what he is *not* doing. He is not doing what Marlowe does. In Marlowe's
Edward II we have a not dissimilar study of a 'weak' King. He, too, is
imprisoned in a dungeon. Here he is, in his misery:

> This dungeon where they keep me is the sink
> Wherein the filth of all the castle falls.
> And there in mire and puddle have I stood
> This ten days' space, and lest that I should sleep
> One plays continually upon a drum.
> They give me bread and water being a king,
> So that for want of sleep and sustenance,
> My mind's distempered, and my body's numbed,
> And whether I have limbs or no I know not.
> O would my blood dropt out from every vein,
> As doth this water from my tatter'd robes.
> Tell Isabel the Queen I look'd not thus,
> When for her sake I ran at tilt in France,
> And there unhors'd the duke of Cleremont.

> (2507)

The conception of tragedy here is diametrically opposed to
Shakespeare's. Shakespeare is not offering a study of degradation and
failure, but one of spiritual advance with courage. Here is Edward's
death:

> *Edward.* Something still buzzeth in mine ears,
> And tells me, if I sleep I never wake.

This fear is that which makes me tremble thus,
And therefore tell me, wherefore art thou come?
   Lightborne. To rid thee of thy life! Matrevis, come!
   Edward. I am too weak and feeble to resist.
Assist me, sweet God, and receive my soul.
   Lightborne. Run for the table.
   Edward. O spare me, or despatch me in a trice.
   Lightborne. So, lay the table down, and stamp on it,
But not too hard, lest that you bruise his body.

(2555)

The death of Barabbas in *The Jew of Malta* is even more undignified;
and that of Faustus in *Doctor Faustus,* though it is given sublime
poetry, remains what I have (in *Shakespearian Production,* enlarged
1964, p.33) called a 'sublime wriggling rather than a sacrificial
suffering'; and he is actually seen being taken off to Hell.

We have an interesting anomaly here. People are made to speak
dramatic poetry for a reason: the poetry at its best is the utterance
of the integral self, or the superself, or soul; and if the poetry is
strong and the protagonist is weak, there is a contradiction that
leaves us dissatisfied. The inmost nature of poetic drama demands
the strength which Shakespeare's tragic heroes illustrate. So now we
have, in contrast to Marlowe, Richard's death:

How now! what means death in this rude assault?
Villain, thine own hand yields thy death's instrument.
                           [*Kills one of his attackers.*]
Go thou and fill another room in hell.
                  [*Killing a second. He is then struck down.*]
That hand shall burn in never-quenching fire
That staggers thus my person. Exton, thy fierce hand
Hath with the king's blood stain'd the king's own land.
Mount, mount my soul! thy seat is up on high,
Whilst my gross flesh sinks downward, here to die.

(V.v.105)

I do not say that Shakespeare is more 'true to life' than Marlowe. He
may, indeed, be less true. I point simply to his tragic conception, which
is concerned less with the appearances of normal life than with the
soul-truth of courage, triumph, and victory-in-death. Richard III thinks

he is bound for Hell; Richard II that he is going to Heaven. That does
not matter: we are not thinking ethically. Both go off in style,
enjoying a state of being which gives them a strange assurance, with
courage in face of death. The word 'soul', important in Shakespeare,
should be duly noted.

The two elements in Richard's story, his intermittent royal
assurance and his growth through depth of suffering, are both present
at his death, with its religious conclusion. Perhaps what we should
most emphasise is his long struggle to adjust himself to the poetry
of kingship, and his final dedication, in death, to himself as king,
which is one with the assurance of his soul's ascent.

In *Richard II* the hero's variations are largely a matter of poetry,
which comes in long speeches, almost 'arias'. In *Romeo and Juliet*
(1595-6) the hero's progress is a progress in the poetry he speaks;
there is a steady advance. On his first entrance he speaks euphuistic
verses of little appeal:

> Why then, O brawling love! O loving hate!
> O any thing! of nothing first create.
> O heavy lightness! serious vanity!
> Mis-shapen chaos of well-seeming forms!
> Feather of lead, bright smoke, cold fire, sick health!
> Still-waking sleep, that is not what it is!
> This love feel I, that feel no love in this.
> Dost thou not laugh?
>
> (I.i.181)

True, the artificiality is intended, and the paradoxes are well
considered:

> Love is a smoke rais'd with the fume of sighs;
> Being purg'd, a fire sparkling in lovers' eyes;
> Being vex'd, a sea nourish'd with lovers' tears.
> What is it else? a madness most discreet,
> A choking gall, and a preserving sweet.
>
> (I.i.196)

Romeo at this stage has no true object for his love; it is all bottled up
inside him, and he therefore speaks the better as a voice of love's
essence and wholeness, seing its paradoxes. These speeches are not all

trivial; they are a kind of prologue to the action. They remain studied, without fervour. His lines on Rosaline do not ring true. She is merely a make-shift, on which to rhapsodise. When he meets Juliet, he speaks with true fervency:

> It seems she hangs upon the cheek of night
> Like a rich jewel in an Ethiop's ear.

(I.v.49)

The sonnet he shares with her in his first approach has charm. In the Balcony scene he unloads passages of imagistic speech that, without being weak, remain somewhat 'operatic'. The language is cut off from the colloquial, it has no accents of normal talk:

> Two of the fairest stars in all the heaven,
> Having some business, do entreat her eyes
> To twinkle in their spheres till they return. . .

(II.ii.15)

Again, watching Juliet as she speaks to herself:

> She speaks:
> O! speak again, bright angel; for thou art
> As glorious to this night, being o'er my head,
> As is a wingèd messenger of heaven
> Unto the white-upturned wondering eyes
> Of mortals, that fall back to gaze on him,
> When he bestrides the lazy-pacing clouds,
> And sails upon the bosom of the air.

(II.ii.25)

Later we have:

> I am no pilot; yet wert thou as far
> As that vast shore wash'd with the furthest sea,
> I would adventure for such merchandise.

(II.ii.82)

While Romeo speaks like this, Juliet's words are far more convincing. She has a sense of the real situation:

> Well, do not swear. Although I joy in thee,
> I have no joy of this contract to-night:
> It is too rash, too unadvis'd, too sudden. . .

> (II.ii.116)

The actor of Romeo feels almost an unfair discrepancy between Juliet's varied utterance, intermixing true love with doubts, poetry with colloquial speech, and his own one-way lines of rhapsodic adoration. While the fictional Romeo rhapsodises, the actor is miserable. It is made more difficult by his having, as a rule, to speak up-stage. The contrast is, however, only an extreme example of Shakespeare's usual treatment of love, in which the woman comes off better than the man. She is real in love; he is a poetic aspirant: we find it again with Orsino and Viola, with Othello and Desdemona. It is almost as though the man loves less a person than love itself. Romeo can even comment on the situation not as a man *in* love but as one speaking *about* a man in love. Hearing Juliet call his name, he says:

> It is my soul that calls upon my name.
> How silver-sweet sound lovers' tongues by night,
> Like softest music to attending ears!

> (II.ii.164)

The loved one is as the lover's soul, his higher self. The succeeding lines are less interesting. It is as though Romeo loves the situation as much as the girl. The hero's task, as we found with Richard II and royalty, is to adjust himself to his own poetry; to make the poetry real. In the Balcony scene it is not quite real, while Juliet's is.

Romeo's secret marriage follows, and then the duelling. Here, for the first time, Romeo has strength. He starts by refusing to meet Tybalt's insulting challenge, for the good reason that Tybalt is now a kinsman, but after Mercutio's death he becomes an avenging fury. He has been too 'effeminate' (III.i.120). Now:

> Away to heaven, respective lenity,
> And fire-ey'd fury be my conduct now!

> (III.i.129)

He rejects 'heaven', and plunges into action. It is a mistake to give him a prolonged fight, or many stabs. In production, Tybalt should stand

amazed, without defence. Romeo vanquishes Tybalt more by the
radiations of his fury than by skill, charging and stabbing in one
wild rush, as may be deduced from his words: 'This shall determine
that' (III.i.137). On the first night of my Toronto 1932 production,
I found that I could not draw my rapier, and had no time to grip
my dagger — or perhaps I had lost it — so I just pushed at Tybalt,
who fell: and the audience, who could not see clearly what was
happening, assumed that he was killed. I did it that way in
subsequent performances; it was true enough to the essence of the
attack. This is a grand moment for the actor: now at last he has
something to grip. Directly after, the spasm over, he knows he is
'fortune's fool' (III.i.142).

The play now jerks forward, there is a new life to it. Half-way
through, the drama, in Shakespeare's usual manner, ignites. In
Romeo's scene with the Friar, where he hears of his banishment, his
abandonment in grief, though somewhat boyish in its petulance, is
yet given impressive sequences:

> There is no world without Verona walls,
> But purgatory, torture, hell itself.
> Hence banishèd is banish'd from the world,
> And world's exile is death; then 'banishèd'
> Is death mis-term'd. Calling death 'banishèd',
> Thou cutt'st my head off with a golden axe,
> And smil'st upon the stroke that murders me.

> (III.iii.17)

The play of words, or thoughts, is still perhaps a trifle artificial, but
it is carried by the prevailing passion. About this there is no doubt:

> Thou canst not speak of that thou dost not feel:
> Wert thou as young as I, Juliet thy love,
> An hour but married, Tybalt murderèd,
> Doting like me, and like me banishèd,
> Then mightst thou speak, then mightst thou tear thy hair,
> And fall upon the ground, as I do now,
> Taking the measure of an unmade grave.

> (III.iii.63)

This is a good example of what may be called 'poetic acting', in which
the whole physique is in attunement with the words. At 'fall upon
the ground', the actor simultaneously falls, and is lying for the last
line, whose accent follows the thought, drawn out as the body lies
full-length, and with a deeper note.

Romeo's poetry is from now on more assured, as though it was
necessary for misfortune to unleash it. He parts with Juliet at dawn:

> It was the lark, the herald of the morn,
> No nightingale: look, love, what envious streaks
> Do lace the severing clouds in yonder east.
> Night's candles are burnt out, and jocund day
> Stands tiptoe on the misty mountain tops:
> I must be gone and live, or stay and die.
>
> (III.v.6)

The apprehension is exquisitely expressed in the imagery; the real dawn
is present, poetically delivered. At 'jocund day' Romeo's eye, for an
instant, lights up: though as a man he is sad, the poetry is bright. In
Shakespeare 'characterisation' is an element in his art, but does not
dominate.

When we next meet Romeo he is in Mantua. He has had a dream that
blends tragedy with joy:

> If I may trust the flattering truth of sleep,
> My dreams presage some joyful news at hand:
> My bosom's lord sits lightly in his throne;
> And all this day an unaccustomed spirit
> Lifts me above the ground with cheerful thoughts.
> I dreamt my lady came and found me dead —
> Strange dream, that gives a dead man leave to think —
> And breath'd such life with kisses in my lips,
> That I reviv'd, and was an emperor.
> Ah me! how sweet is love itself possess'd,
> When but love's shadows are so rich in joy!
>
> (V.i.1)

He is half in a spirit-existence: 'spirit' lifts him 'above the ground'. The
dream is one of death and revival through love, and he becomes an
'emperor', the word denoting a new life of immeasurable richness.

We think of 'an emperor Antony' in Cleopatra's dream (*Antony and Cleopatra*, V.ii.76), and of the last plays. We have a glimpse of a truth beyond tragedy.

The hope of joyful news may be thought ironic, in view of what follows; but it is only superficially so, because the news is, in a way, good. I mean this. Romeo hears from his servant Balthasar of Juliet's supposed death. He greets the news not with misery or anguish, but with defiance. The news jerks him many stages up his ladder of poetic advance:

> Is it even so? Then I defy you, stars!
>
> (V.i.24)

He follows on with words of sudden purpose and efficiency:

> Thou know'st my lodging: get me ink and paper,
> And hire post-horses; I will hence to-night.
>
> (V.i.25)

His servant fears his wild looks: but there is an over-riding calmness and determination. Here Romeo, as Granville-Barker says, 'comes to his full height' (*Preface to Romeo and Juliet,* 'Characters').

This is the first time Romeo has spoken of practical details: we are within a new poetic realism. Also he is manly; on the stage he should be wearing riding boots, and a long cloak. He has a new dignity, and his voice should reflect it. For the actor, it is all most enjoyable; the part really never catches fire till the news of Juliet's death. As tragedy thickens round the protagonist, the actor's enjoyment increases, and this pleasure in the acting reflects a meaning. We may say that the actor enjoys the poetic dimension of what is being performed; or, to preserve the fiction's realism, that he enacts the over-soul of the protagonist, which remains unruffled, 'tempest-tost' as in *Macbeth* (I.iii.24-5), but not 'lost'. Romeo may be unhappy, but his over-soul, which is the poetry, enjoys itself mightily.

He next describes the Apothecary:

> . . .meagre were his looks,
> Sharp misery had worn him to the bones. . .
>
> (V.i.40)

He describes the shop with its jumble of goods; and the
Apothecary's 'penury'. Romeo has hitherto thought only of
himself. But he has grown up — 'shot up' would be more true — since
the news of Juliet's death, and he now speaks, like Richard II in his
meditative soliloquy, as one objectively aware of general human
suffering, unrelated to himself. The Apothecary — a wonderful part
on the stage — is suffering personified, and acts here as the implement
of tragedy. Romeo asks for poison:

> *Apothecary.* Such mortal drugs I have; but Mantua's law
> Is death to any he that utters them.
> *Romeo.* Art thou so bare, and full of wretchedness,
> And fear'st to die? Famine is in thy cheeks,
> Need and oppression starveth in thine eyes,
> Contempt and beggary hang upon thy back;
> The world is not thy friend, nor the world's law:
> The world affords no law to make thee rich;
> Then be not poor, but break it, and take this.
> *Apothecary.* My poverty, but not my will, consents.
> *Romeo.* I pay thy poverty, and not thy will.
> *Apothecary.* Put this in any liquid thing you will,
> And drink it off; and if you had the strength
> Of twenty men, it would dispatch you straight.
> *Romeo.* There is thy gold, worse poison to men's souls,
> Doing more murders in this loathsome world,
> Than these poor compounds that thou may'st not sell:
> I sell thee poison, thou has sold me none.
>
> (V.i.66)

He is however genuinely pained by the Apothecary's destitution, and his
words are warm with sympathy. A gesture, such as the laying of his
hand on his shoulder, is indicated:

> Farewell; buy food, and get thyself in flesh.
> Come, cordial and not poison, go with me
> To Juliet's grave, for there must I use thee.
>
> (V.i.83)

Romeo is in a new consciousness. He is aware of suffering humanity,
and even sees the world as 'loathsome'. Law-breaking is not merely
allowed; it is right. He is socially nihilistic, but out of that nihilism

flowers a superb truth, or half-truth: 'I sell thee poison, thou hast sold me none.' He is in the world of *Timon of Athens*. All this may be 'out of character'. That Romeo should suddenly attain such tragic dignity may seem illogical; but it is what the poetry says. What we have been watching is a drama of poetic development with a basis in 'ordinary' life but not controlled by it.*

He enters the tomb. He dismisses his servant, Balthasar, giving the man a letter for his father. Though set on a terrible purpose, he is utterly responsible, and not mad, though a burning ferocity is in him, if need be:

> . . .therefore hence, be gone:
> But, if thou, jealous, dost return to pry
> In what I further shall intend to do,
> By heaven, I will tear thee joint by joint,
> And strew this hungry churchyard with thy limbs.

(V.iii.32)

Assured that Balthasar will not remain, he speaks kindly, and gives him money, like Timon with Flavius:

> So shalt thou show me friendship. Take thou that:
> Live and be prosperous; and farewell, good fellow.

(V.iii.41)

He next meets the hostile Paris, but is unwilling to hurt him: 'Good gentle youth, tempt not a desperate man' (V.iii.59). 'Youth': Romeo speaks as one of an older generation. He advises Paris to fly from a 'madman' (V.iii.67); but, his words being ineffectual, they fight, and Paris is slain. He takes his hand in death, and, with no thought of rivalry, will 'bury' him near Juliet.

The end is approached calmly, with thoughts of happiness before death, at first doubted, but then half-ratified by sight of Juliet, who seems so unnaturally bright in death's despite:

---

*One might compare Aristotle's statement in the *Poetics* that in tragedy *action* takes precedence over *character*. For the subtleties involved in Aristotle's contention, see B.R. Rees, 'Plot, Character and Thought', *Le Monde Grec,* Université Libre de Bruxelles, 1975.

> How oft when men are at the point of death
> Have they been merry! which their keepers call
> A lightning before death: O! how may I
> Call this a lightning? O my love! my wife!
> Death, that hath suck'd the honey of thy breath,
> Hath had no power yet upon thy beauty:
> Thou art not conquer'd; beauty's ensign yet
> Is crimson in thy lips and in thy cheeks,
> And death's pale flag is not advancèd there.
>
> (V.iii.88)

What has happened? He is amazed and in momentary joy at Juliet's
seeming life. The beauty of the poetry reflects a truth, for Romeo,
as in his recent dream, is being again attuned to an intuition beyond
death: that is why the lines ring in us with so great an appeal. At this
last moment, Romeo is exactly measured to his own poetry; the
adjustment is perfected. He has climbed his hill.

He sees Tybalt's body, and asks forgiveness — 'Forgive me, cousin' —
for having 'cut thy youth in twain' (V.iii.99); again an emphasis, as
Granville-Barker notes, on the other's 'youth'. He is in a state of supreme
understanding above mortal conflicts. He embraces and kisses Juliet
as a wedding-in-death, and takes the poison:

> Come, bitter conduct, come unsavoury guide!
> Thou desperate pilot, now at once run on
> The dashing rocks thy sea-sick weary bark!
> Here's to my love! O true apothecary!
> Thy drugs are quick. Thus with a kiss I die.
>
> (V.iii.116)

The 'pilot' may be compared with his former reference, seeing himself
as venturing across seas for love's 'merchandise' (page 38). His quest
is now different; or perhaps the same.

Juliet's death is given only a few lines and is done perfunctorily.
Women in Shakespeare, supreme in love, are not accorded tragic
dignity. Juliet's fine potion speech (IV.iii.14-59), with its terror,
would not be allowed for a man.

Once again, all this is enjoyable for the actor. From the news of
Juliet's death on, Romeo is a tragic protagonist of power, and in
the process much of obvious splendour attends. He is aware of

suffering, and is kindly to the Apothecary and Balthasar; and is in a state transcending former enmities, forgiving, and all but loving, Paris and Tybalt; but he is also wild with a controlled and purposeful passion. He has grown up many years; indeed, being death shadowed, an eternity. He speaks supreme poetry at sight of Juliet in her strange life. Such is Romeo's triumph: we have nothing to regret, and much to acclaim.

3 ON POETIC ACTING

In our time we have heard much, from T.S. Eliot and others, of the
'dissociation of sensibility', which is supposed to have dated from the
seventeenth century. What is meant is the split between intellect and
emotion, which may also take the form of the opposition of reason
and occult recognition. Pope was aware of the disruption in his plea
for acceptance of instinct as against reason in Epistles II and III of his
Essay on Man; while at the conclusion to *The Dunciad* he foresees the
breakdown of our culture coming about through this very split. It is
sometimes assumed that this split has invalidated all our endeavours,
including subsequent poetry; but this is a grave error, for wherever
poetry has been authentic we have a healing of the wound. This is,
indeed, what poetry is *for:* to heal the wound, which has in fact
existed long before the seventeenth century, dating back to the
origins of the intellect.

When making the persons of his drama speak in poetry, the poet is
making them, heroes and lesser persons alike, speak from beyond this
'dissociation of sensibility', and therefore, in part, from a height
overlooking their immediate concerns. It can happen in a prose play
too: as Bernard Shaw said towards the end of his preface to *Saint Joan*,
the people are made to speak as if they realised, as the real persons
would not have realised, the further implications of their actions:
'The things I represent these three exponents of the drama as saying
are the things they actually would have said if they had known what
they were really doing.' According to Granville-Barker, people in
poetic drama have to express both what is known to them and also
truths about themselves they do '*not* know'; all of which things,
diverse and sometimes contradictory, must be expressed at one and the
same time' and 'in one and the same fashion' (*On Poetry in Drama*,
Romanes Lecture 1937, p.34). This concentration is not on external
character, but on the 'hidden man' (*Collected Prefaces to Shakespeare*
1958, vol.I, p.7.)

That Shakespeare's dramatic poetry entwines so regularly the
colloquial with the rhetorical establishes a needed relation with
ordinary life so that we are invited to participate in a progress from
normal behaviour patterns towards what may be termed a 'higher

consciousness': or even a higher common sense. With Shakespeare's heroes this higher consciousness is not only present in the poetry, but the nature and use of it is carefully, as it were, exposed before us. The heroes not only see themselves as the action matures with a new clarity, but also become more objectively philosophic and self-less, while through that very selflessness a new thing, which we may call the 'soul', is being born. At the opening of his *Preface to Hamlet*, Granville-Barker sees Shakespeare's imagination beginning to give his persons, through their poetry, something 'like an immortal soul'.

Such a view of poetry makes strong demands on the imagination; and the best way to vitalise the imagination is through the art of public reading. Without that it will remain undeveloped. Educationally what we have to do is draw out, educe, from the student powers usually dormant. So the sensitive teacher will do well to alert his students to the infinite variety of intonation needed for the speaking of Shakespeare; or indeed poetry in general. He may be receptive to advice, and proceed, as he thinks, to implement it. Here however there is a catch. He may not be able to hear what he is actually doing. I mean, he may well think he is expressing the needed variations; they are in his head, and in speaking he hears them, as it were, within his head; but they are not being projected to the hearer outside. The only way to bring this home to him is to get him to listen to his own speaking on a tape; and he may then be shocked to discover how little he is conveying of the variegated powers he thought that he was expressing.

He may raise objections. He may say, 'The meaning is in the words; surely all one wants to do is to speak them audibly, and the audience will respond. We do not want to be accused of gilding the lily.' One fallacy here is obvious: what audience is he thinking of? People in one room? People in a hall? In a large theatre? Correct speaking will vary the emphasis far more powerfully for a large audience than a small one, and without such variation he will not grip them; or even be audible, since audibility depends very largely on the audience getting the phrase units and not only the words, and feeling the relevant meanings. There is another difficulty. He may be reluctant to delve into his deeper self and draw from it the emotional resources that are needed; he may have inhibitions about getting the required tones and resonance, thinking them too emotional, or put otherwise, fearing to reveal the soul of the poetry, as something almost indecent. The answer to this is clear. Suggest to the student that he may well be right, and say that he can, if he likes, so speak the lines. But ask him first to speak them with full depth and variation, to show that he *can* do it; and let him hear the result. If it is negative, the obvious implication is that his excuses are merely a veil to his real reasons: the inability to speak his lines correctly.

I cannot over-emphasise the value for the student in imaginative apprehension of a series of such trials; if he draws out from himself the richer music of speech, he will begin to enjoy the use of powers hitherto dormant and will advance in his understanding of literature. If he fails, he will remain, to that extent, in an unimaginative state. I believe the answer to many of our literary problems in education is to be found in making the student listen to records of his own voice.

An easy way to see what may be demanded is to consider certain of Shakespeare's longer speeches, and see how they build up and flower in the process.* As a start, I point to the King's sleep-speech in *2 Henry IV* (III.i.4-31). The King is at first weak, through sleeplessness:

> How many thousand of my poorest subjects
> Are at this hour asleep! O sleep! O gentle sleep!
> Nature's soft nurse, how have I frighted thee,
> That thou no more wilt weigh my eyelids down
> And steep my senses in forgetfulness?

The voice breaks; he is almost in tears. He next reasons, with a firmer voice:

> Why rather, sleep, liest thou in smoky cribs,
> Upon uneasy pallets stretching thee,
> And hush'd with buzzing night-flies to thy slumber,
> Than in the perfum'd chambers of the great,
> Under the canopies of costly state,

---

*I have often made these the subject of a lecture, as printed in *The City of London School Chronicle*, Vol.I, No.2, July 1970. The readings were broadcast, under the title 'Shakespeare's Rhetoric', on the BBC (1963, repeated 1964). There is a tape of them made by Sound Seminars, Cincinnati; and marketed until recently by McGraw-Hill in New York and England, but they have now been transferred to Jeffrey Norton, Publishers, Inc., 145 East 49th Street, New York.

> And lull'd with sound of sweetest melody?
> O thou dull god! Why liest thou with the vile
> In loathsome beds, and leav'st the kingly couch
> A watch-case or a common 'larum bell?

That is comparatively straight-forward, and will be spoken normally, though with a momentary access of vocal grandeur for the 'perfum'd chambers'. But now the speech starts to burgeon out, to flower:

> Wilt thou upon the high and giddy mast
> Seal up the ship-boy's eyes, and rock his brains
> In cradle of the rude imperious surge,
> And in the visitation of the winds,
> Who take the ruffian billows by the top,
> Curling their monstrous heads, and hanging them
> With deaf'ning clamour in the slippery clouds,
> That with the hurly death itself awakes?

Sleep is a great power, by hyperbole imagined here as a yet greater power than death; as indeed it may be, or as great anyway, since we do not know what sleep is, or where we go to in sleep; perhaps to the Elysian fields of death itself. Such thoughts multiply from inspection of the poetry. But what of the sleepless King and his broken voice? We have completely forgotten them. The actor will be concentrating only on the poetry, and giving it all the strength at his disposal. The fourth line here goes quickly, but we slow down for the fifth, the voice rising on 'top'. From 'curling' to 'slippery clouds' a maximum of power will be needed, an especially heavy stress falling on the delaying and obstructive syllables of 'deafening clamour', followed in the next line by an awed quiet, for death itself.

Now the speech continues, still quiet, and a little wistful, for what follows:

> Canst thou, O partial sleep! give thy repose
> To the wet sea-boy in an hour so rude,
> And in the calmest and most stillest night,
> With all appliances and means to boot,
> Deny it to a King?

We can enjoy the second vowel of 'repòse', which speaks volumes;

and also the phrase 'wet sea-boy', accenting 'bòy'. And so to the final couplet:

> Then, happy low, lie down!
> Uneasy lies the head that wears a crown.

We return to the quiet accents of the opening, after our tumultuous adventure. But this is the point I would drive home: the psychological situation gives birth to a poetic splendour, which in manner of execution has little in common with the psychological situation we started with.

This build-up is usual in Shakespeare's long speeches. We have it in *Richard II* in John O'Gaunt's 'This royal throne of kings' speech (II.i.40-68), where colloquial intonations should allow for an old man's quavering repetitions:

> This royal throne of kings, this scepter'd isle,
> This earth of majesty, this seat of Mars,
> This other Eden, demi-paradise,
> This fortress built by Nature for herself
> Against infection and the hand of war,
> This happy breed of men, this little world,
> This precious stone set in the silver sea,
> Which serves it in the office of a wall,
> Or as a moat defensive to a house,
> Against the envy of less happier lands;
> This blessed plot, this earth, this realm, this England,
> This nurse, this teeming womb of royal kings,
> Fear'd by their breed and famous by their birth,
> Renownèd for their deeds as far from home —
> For Christian service and true chivalry —
> As is the sepulchre in stubborn Jewry
> Of the world's ransom, blessèd Mary's Son:
> This land of such dear souls, this dear, dear land,
> Dear for her reputation, through the world,
> Is now leas'd out — I die pronouncing it —
> Like to a tenement, or pelting farm. . .

We may be excused for wondering whether the old man will ever get to the point. He repeats himself rather like Polonius, though the characterisation of age must not be overdone, or it spoils the content; a reminder here and there is probably enough. There is a purpose in it all, over and above the 'characterisation'. England's glory has been defined, almost over-defined, and then a new voice takes over:

> England, bound in with the triumphant sea,
> Whose rocky shore beats back the envious siege
> Of watery Neptune, is now bound in with shame,
> With inky blots, and rotten parchment bonds:
> That England, that was wont to conquer others,
> Hath made a shameful conquest of itself.

We forget about the 'characterisation'. All the compacted force possible is needed for the scorn of 'inky blots and rotten parchment bonds'; and then the final, sedate and withering judgement. All the pauses, withdrawings and repetitions of the earlier lines are preparatory to, and built into, this ending.

We have this kind of thing often. Henry V's 'Crispin' speech starts weakly, talking of honour with a seemingly deliberate lack of conviction, until it takes fire at 'This day is called the Feast of Crispian'. On the stage, King Henry probably finds the name when looking over some papers, to which he has turned in embarrassment at finding his first words inadequate. The reaction of those around him, first in doubt, and gradually enthusiasm, should be evident. The *name* is so important that the speech finally doubles it, in:

> And Crispin Crispian shall ne'er go by,
> From this day to the ending of the world,
> But we in it shall be rememberèd. . .

> > *(Henry V,* IV.iii.57)

We may almost say that, so far as the play is concerned, the Battle of Agincourt was won by the poetic radiations of the word 'Crispin'. Its sound obliquely suggests 'Christian'.

A particularly fine example of the build-up towards revelation occurs in *Antony and Cleopatra* (IV.xii.35-54). Antony has just heard of Cleopatra's supposed death. He speaks in turn to Eros, his armour-bearer, to Mardian who has brought the news, to himself, to his armour, and to Cleopatra. Note that after 'battery' we understand 'coming':

Unarm, Eros; the long day's task is done,
And we must sleep. [*To Mardian*] That thou depart'st hence safe,
Does pay thy labour richly; go. [*To Eros*] Off, pluck off!
The seven-fold shield of Ajax cannot keep
The battery from my heart. O! cleave my sides,
Heart, once be stronger than the continent,
Crack thy frail case! Apace, Eros, apace.
No more a soldier; bruisèd pieces, go;
You have been nobly borne. From me awhile. [*Exit Eros*]
I will o'ertake thee, Cleopatra, and
Weep for my pardon.

Though the disjointed addresses all radiate from his concern at the news, which is central to them, they remain disjointed. Now he indulges in a complex thought:

So it must be, for now
All length is torture; since the torch is out,
Lie down, and stray no further. Now all labour
Mars what it does; yea, very force entangles
Itself with strength; seal then, and all is done.

Temporal existence has become unbearable; life is self-contradictory; force of biological existence is mastered by the 'strength' of spiritual compulsion. So to the climax, in utter simplicity:

Eros! — I come, my queen — Eros! — Stay for me:
Where souls do couch on flowers, we'll hand in hand,
And with our sprightly port make the ghosts gaze;
Dido and her Aeneas shall want troops,
And all the haunt be ours. Come, Eros! Eros!

He wants Eros to come and kill him. See how the germ of Elysian expectation flowers out. The speech starts with abrupt addresses, follows up with complex thought, and then comes the resolving and revelatory climax.

It is a matter pre-eminently of poetry. The distinctions I have been making through this book, and the qualities I have been defining, are poetic, and without close attention to the poetry we shall not be aware of them.

That is why my thesis is far more convincing when spoken than when written, despite what has to be omitted. Such, then, is the challenge to the actor. If Richard III does not strike a deeper note for his 'foreboding' speeches, or if Romeo does not use a fitting register in his fifth act and stride about the stage with a new dignity, probably slower, as though weighted with the world's sufferings, and yet dynamic too, we shall not interpret what the poetry offers us.

This means that the actor should act not the character alone, but the poetry; and especially toward the close, the poetry more than the character. Bernard Shaw has a helpful comment here. Mrs Patrick Campbell once asked him for help in respect to the character of Lady Macbeth, and he replied:

> When you play Shakespeare, don't worry about the character, but go for the music. It was by word music that he expressed what he wanted to express; and if you get the music right, the whole thing will come right. And neither he nor any other musician ever wrote music without *fortissimi* and thundering ones too. It is only your second rate people who write whole movements for muted strings and never let the trombones and the big drums go. . .If you want to know the truth about Lady Macbeth's character, she hasn't one. There never was no such person. She says things that will set people's imagination to work if she says them in the right way; that is all. . .
>
> (*Bernard Shaw and Mrs Patrick Campbell: their correspondence,* ed. Alan Dent, 1952, pp.218-19.)

'There never was no such person': that is true. Lady Macbeth exists in the realm of fiction, and so do all the people and events in Shakespeare; but the poetry is a present reality to be experienced by us in a way that the rest cannot be. Shaw's words may be an overstatement, but it is an overstatement that makes an all-important point. I myself found Macbeth a not too arduous part to perform for the very reason that so much depends on the poetry. A.C. Bradley's fine study of *Macbeth* is mainly a study in poetic psychology; it was bound to be that. Therefore performance, given a just poetic projection, is comparatively simple. The sharp interchanges of *Othello* and *King Lear* are more demanding; the poetry has more variation, and you have to consider other performers.

It is not quite so obvious as Bernard Shaw implies. The just speaking

of the poetry is not at all easy, nor is it only the speaking of the
poetry, but the acting of it, that is required. I gave an example
in my discussion of *Romeo and Juliet,* where Romeo's fall matched
his verse (page 41 above). That was a very obvious example, but it
should happen, or be ready to happen, all the time, in subtle, or at
choice moments extreme, ways. What we should be doing is
performing the part not of an ordinary man, but of a poetic man. I
have recently twice been pained by performances of Hamlet by
eminent young actors. The verse was split up quite intolerably. I do
not suggest that they were impervious to the poetry, or unable to
speak it: they were just aiming at the wrong thing. Faced by the
complexities of Hamlet, and his various worryings and muddles, they
thought, 'How should such a man speak?' Obviously, they concluded,
in a muddled fashion. The result was a sequence of discontinuities
and jolts. Instead, they should have regarded their task as one
presenting a man who says things like:

> The undiscover'd country, from whose bourn
> No traveller returns. . .

(III.i.79)

And

> Absent thee from felicity awhile,
> And in this harsh world draw thy breath in pain.

(V.ii.361)

Hamlet as a 'character' may be confused, but his poetry is not; he is
less a 'character' than a poetic voice, speaking from a height overlooking
his problems. That is our primary fact. It may be untrue to life; people
do not speak like that, but there it is, and we have to make what we
can of it. If we succeed, we end up by having a supreme experience.

When Shakespeare wants a realistic utterance, he uses prose, as in
Hamlet's Nunnery dialogue with Ophelia (III.i.90-158). It is also true
that he can endue prose with poetic properties, as in his lines on the
heavenly firmament (II.ii.311-31).

All the obvious reservations are admitted. It is as important to
intershade the colloquial accents as to do justice to the poetic. In
his 'Seneca in Elizabethan Translation' (*Selected Essays 1917-1932*
p.91), T.S. Eliot describes how the Elizabethans learned from
Seneca the skills of declamation: 'The art of dramatic language, we

must remember, is as near to oratory as to ordinary speech or to other poetry'. But they did not stop there: 'Their subsequent progress is a process of splitting up the primitive rhetoric, developing out of it subtler poetry and subtler tones of conversation, eventually mingling, as no other school of dramatists has done, the oratorical, the conversational, the elaborate and the simple, the direct and the indirect; so that they were able to write plays which can still be viewed as plays, with any plays, and which can still be read as poetry, with any poetry'. There is a continual interaction. I have often drawn attention, as an example, to Hamlet's words to his mother:

> Look here, upon this picture and on this:
> The counterfeit presentment of two brothers.
> See, what a grace was seated on this brow:
> Hyperion's curls, the front of Jove himself,
> An eye like Mars to threaten and command,
> A station like the herald Mercury
> New-lighted on a heaven-kissing hill.
> A combination and a form indeed
> Where every god did seem to set his seal,
> To give the world assurance of a man.

> (III.iv.53)

It starts colloquially, more or less, but in the third line rises. After that, the quality of each god is to be reflected not only in the voice but in the eye and facial expression of the actor, with swift changes that yet do not impede the poetic flow. At 'A combination' we return to a more colloquial utterance. It is like an aeroplane, taking off for flight, and returning to the ground.

Shaw's advice to attend to the 'music' is good, but the word 'music' contains manifold implications: vowel-colouring, vocal height or depth, according to the quality of the thought expressed; and alteration of speed, with continual variation between the colloquial and the rhetorical, and between natural stress and metrical beat; and all in strict obedience moreover to the things and qualities which the poetry, moment by moment, handles; and all flowing spontaneously;*

---

*For spontaneity as 'a constant factor in theatre art', see Richard Courtney, 'Theatre and Spontaneity', *The Journal of Aesthetics and Art Criticism,* XXXII.1; Fall, 1973 (USA).

and all distinctly audible. I say 'distinctly', since it is not enough to ask
a member of the audience, 'Could you hear that?' What one should ask
is, 'Could you hear that without straining?' Any effort devoted to
listening takes from the psychic resources needed for the audience's
enjoyment and experience.

The language, too, must be not only spoken but lived. T.S. Eliot,
in his essay on Seneca (page 55 above) writes well of Greek tragedy,
whose physical actuality he contrasts (p.68) with Seneca's verbal art:

> Behind the drama of words is the drama of action, the timbre of
> voice and voice, the uplifted hand or tense muscle, and the
> particular emotion. The spoken play, the words which we read, are
> symbols, a shorthand, and often, as in the best of Shakespeare, a
> very abbreviated shorthand indeed, for the acted and felt play, which
> is always the real thing. The phrase, beautiful as it may be, stands
> for a greater beauty still.

The physical and emotional elements are felt as constituent to a
'greater beauty' than the words alone: though the words are there
too, to give them point and meaning.

When Hamlet in soliloquy says:

> And can say nothing – no, not for a king
> Upon whose property and most dear life
> A damn'd defeat was made.

                                                                    (II.ii.604)

his eye should momentarily light up and his face glow for the memory
of his Father, and then cloud quickly for the 'damned defeat'. Such a
lightning transition would be impossible in normal behaviour. The
poetry directing us, we make a leap of imaginative apprehension to what
is behind the poetry;* as Richard II has it (page 33 above), the externals
of first facial expression and gesture and next of words – for gesture
tends to precede speech – are no better than 'shadows' of the soul-reality
within. That soul-reality we should intuit and from that soul-reality we
should, as actors, work. This is what I mean by acting the kind of man –

---

*For an interesting discussion of what is sometimes called the 'sub-text', that is,
the underlying significances of dramatic speech, see John Russell Brown,
Shakespeare's Plays in Performance (1966), IV.

he has never actually existed, of course – who speaks in poetry.

At choice moments – not always, necessarily – the actor's broader gestures should be made to correspond closely to the verse. *Othello* provides an example:

> *Iago.* Patience, I say: your mind perhaps may change.
> *Othello.* Never Iago. Like to the Pontic Sea
> Whose icy current and compulsive course
> Ne'er feels retiring ebb, but keeps due on
> To the Propontic and the Hellespont,
> Even so. . .

(III.iv.453)

At this crest of passion Othello has, we may suppose, his hand out. It is then drawn across, imitating the course of the sea being described; but it must be timed exactly to correspond to the three and a half lines, finishing with them. Though a passionate speech, it must be disciplined in the action, and the passion carried into the extended simile. This does not mean that gestures should be found to illustrate everything. I once heard an actor illustrate Richard II's

> With mine own tears I wash away my balm

(IV.i.207)

by pointing to his eyes; which struck me as unnecessary. Wide gestures should be used with reserve.

I adduce two authorities to make my argument clearer. One is from George Henry Lewes, writing in the last century of Salvini's Othello:

> I remember nothing so musically perfect in its *tempo* and intonation, so emotionally perfect in expression, as his delivery of this passage – the fury visibly growing with every word, his whole being vibrating, his face aflame, the voice becoming more and more terrible, and yet so completely under musical control that it never approached a scream.
>
> (*On Actors and the Art of Acting,* 1875, p.269)

The concluding words are important: it is a highly disciplined business; though 'control' may not be the right word, unless, as here, it is grouped with 'musical'. The actor's voice should never shout, unless a shout, as a shout, is particularly demanded. Its volume and intensity should compass the needed power without that; and indeed, it will be a greater power, since a shout has none, or little. Observe that the whole body is being used. Poetic acting is not a matter solely of voice, face and hands. The best way to see what this means is to study the various pictures of Beerbohm Tree (page 172 below); see also my *Shakespearian Production* (enlarged, 1964). I have presented a full study of bodily action in *Symbol of Man*, still unpublished.

My other authority is the French actor, Jean-Louis Barrault:

> In writing his tragedies Racine obeyed the exacting demands of Number and pure geometry. The virtues essential to a classical work are Measure and Design.
>
> The actor, too, does his best to obey Number in his diction. At all events, he recognises it. Moreover his conduct has to be in accordance with that imposed by the author. Hence both in his actions and in his speech he does not conduct himself in an ordinary way.
>
> Up to this point, then, the purity of dramatic art is safeguarded. The language is elliptic, the action 'crystallised.' If this purity is to be absolutely safeguarded the actor must also move in a way that is not ordinary. His gesticulation, like the alexandrines he utters and the conduct he pursues, must be calculated, chosen, rhythmic. If this is not so, what happens?
>
> Any transition from gesture to speech becomes impossible, for a synthesis of what is seen and what is heard cannot take place. The 'chemical precipitate' of this delicate artistic operation cannot come about. The theatrical phenomenon ceases to exist. We no longer know where we are. If we think we are in ordinary life, then we wonder why the characters speak and conduct themselves in such an extraordinary way. If, on the other hand, we persist in our idea that the stage is a magical place, a mysterious casket of illusions, then it disturbs us to see such ordinary characters moving about on it.
>
> It is because of this sudden weakness that many people think the theatre an impure art, vulgar and second rate.
>
> The public, accustomed to plastic naturalism, is usually bored by tragedy; it falls asleep to the rhythm of the alexandrines. But what it should do is to hoot at the 'false notes' traced in the air by actors ignorant of gesticulation, just as it would hoot with

horror on hearing a discordant orchestra.

An actor who wants to acquire the science of gesticulation, who wants to learn how to calculate, select, and make rhythmic a gesture-language that will harmonize with the spoken language composed by the author, must submit to a training in formation and suppleness.

(Reflection on the Theatre, tr. Barbara Wall, 1951; II.iii.pp.113-14)

I do not assume that what is true for Racine's alexandrines will be always suitable for Shakespeare's verse, though Barrault's argument holds for much of Shakespeare. Shakespeare adds a dimension of complexity in his variation between colloquial accent and metrical beat; the art of speaking Shakespearian verse exists in this very play, together with variation in pace and much else. The actor will vary ordinary behaviour, for much of the time, with a more poetic, or symbolic, action. Shakespeare's use of prose indicates how nearly he approaches, when he wishes to, normal behaviour, and much of the verse demands nothing excessively grandiose. But it should be ready for it when it comes, and the total performance should be coloured by imaginative apprehensions.

4 TRANSITION

After his early histories Shakespeare wrote the two parts of *Henry IV* (1595-7). In these there is no tragic hero, but Falstaff dominates. Though he is a comedic figure he has serious aspects: his speech on 'Honour' in Part I (V.i.128-43) and on Sherris-sack in Part II (IV.iii.92-136) have forceful and direct meanings. As his story develops, he becomes, as Dover Wilson showed in *The Fortunes of Falstaff*, less comic and more powerful. This change corresponds to the advances we have noted in other heroes. He is given a moving love scene to music (*2 Henry IV*, II.iv.244-52) and is respected as a soldier (IV.iii.18). He is being taken more seriously, and becomes dangerous to those around, acting as a satiric and disruptive threat to his society; so that he has, necessarily, to be rejected by his former companion, now King Henry V. He is however sympathetically conceived throughout; and the description of his death is impressive (*Henry V*, II.iii.7-41).

Beside Falstaff we can place Shylock in *The Merchant of Venice* (about 1597). He is ambiguously treated in the early scenes, as a mixture of cunning and racial dignity. When his daughter and much of his wealth are stolen from him he is subjected to cruel comedy by the Christians, and speaks nobly in his race's defence. After that, we are prepared for his revenge on Antonio. In the Court scene he for the first time has a long and fully developed verse-speech; it conforms to Shakespeare's usual manner, with a suspended movement gathering to a good climax. What is strange, however, is its content. Instead of saying that his daughter and riches have been stolen from him, and that he accordingly cannot be expected to forgive; or that Antonio had been in the habit of spitting on him in public; instead of this, he bases his case on an irrational loathing on his own part which he cannot describe further. He takes his stand on personal and presumably racial antipathy, and nothing but that. It is as though he has reached an impersonal truth, to which all other arguments are subsidiary. To this extent he conforms to the advance we have noticed in Shakespeare's tragic heroes.

These two, Falstaff and Shylock, stand out. They are both outsiders in their respective societies, and may be said to continue the tradition of earlier heroes. Shylock compacts a maximum of realism; I sometimes think that it is the best thing in the tragic vein that Shakespeare ever did. Beside these two we might place Malvolio in *Twelfth Night* (about 1601), whose egotism and ambition are punished by mocking and suspected madness, from which he emerges to denounce his enemies and leave them, with a regained dignity.

Unrestful powers are working in Shakespeare's dramaturgy. Shylock nearly ruins his play. It would seem that Shakespeare must have been aware of this, and aware too of the mysterious power generated in his early tragic works. What *was* this power? What were these near supermen? What did they mean? And were they good or evil? Or did that not matter?

In *Julius Caesar* (1599) he attempts to create a wholly good, or at least honourable, tragic hero in the noble Brutus, but somehow the attempt does not quite succeed. Despite fine moments, the result is static. Some element of *growth* appears to be necessary, and that means some element of guilt or folly to start with; and that is why, while Brutus remains static, Cassius, starting as a schemer, almost with the attributes of a stage villain, subsequently falls into line with Shakespeare's tragic heroes, and, from the Quarrel scene until his death, races ahead, dies for a friend, and is crowned, like Cleopatra, in death. Brutus' death is comparatively dull. Apart from this, the political nature of the play, containing as it does no less than four leading figures, scarcely lends itself to a tragic form.

Having written this, I find an apposite passage in Henri Suhamy's 'Guilt and Retribution in *Julius Caesar*' (Agrégation, University of Paris, 1974). He finds, justly I think, an element of undefined guilt in Brutus, but he stresses a conclusion for both Brutus and Cassius in line with my present essay:

Yet we would perhaps miss some essential dimension of the play if we should conceive the catharsis of Cassius and Brutus crowning up the tragedy as mere humbling down of the soul before the severity of Fate. To them failure does not amount to condemnation. It is surprisingly just before they die that Cassius and Brutus assert themselves and voice their stoic pride with the firmest alacrity. Neither in Cassius' nor in Brutus' dying speeches do we feel any regret for what they have done. Indeed they have reached catharsis, that is to say, purgation of the passions. Cassius is purged of his hatred and of his activistic worldliness. Brutus is purged of his ambition and of his smugness. But even though they admit that a debt had to be paid and a game lost, they are purged of their guilty feelings too. They have come to a paradoxical and lofty awareness that through their struggles and dilemmas they have lived a noble and unique experience. . .They have assured the survival of the values which they fought and perished for, indeed their own survival.

It could not have been said better.

And now for *Hamlet* (about 1601). Shakespeare sets himself to the tragic enigma, and *Hamlet* is less a tragedy than a play about tragedy, studying it from all angles. Hamlet is aware of tragedy from the beginning; he starts where other tragic heroes leave off. The objective and impersonal survey touched by the tragic heroes in their last scenes is in Hamlet throughout. He has two primary objective interests. One is Death. Death, which is an aspect of tragedy, over-arches the whole action. Hamlet converses with the Ghost of his Father, and from then on we are never far from it: in Hamlet's soliloquys, the deaths of Polonius and Ophelia, the elaborated words of Hamlet to the King concerning putrifying corpses, his graveyard meditations, and the accumulation of dead bodies at the end, with Fortinbras':

> O proud death!
> What feast is toward in thine eternal cell,
> That thou so many princes at a shot
> So bloodily hath struck?
>
> (V.ii.378)

Hamlet is a play largely about death, and Hamlet, as a man, is throughout concerned with it.

To turn to the second of Hamlet's objective and impersonal interests: dramatic art in relation to life. Hamlet hears the Player speak a tragic speech, and soliloquises at length about the relation of the Player's artistry to his own situation. He plans to have a play performed imitating the King's crime, and discusses with the Players the technique of acting; appearing in fact to be far more interested in this, as no doubt was Shakespeare too, than in his plot to catch the King. The Player had earlier spoken emotionally, and his emotion is to be contrasted with Hamlet's own speaking, which had more 'discretion' (II.ii.498). Hamlet accordingly counsels temperance:

Speak the speech, I pray you, as I pronounced it to you, trippingly on
the tongue; but if you mouth it, as many of your players do, I had
as lief the town-crier spoke my lines. Nor do not saw the air too
much with your hand, thus; but use all gently, for in the very torrent,
tempest, and – as I may say – whirlwind of passion, you must
acquire and beget a temperance, that may give it smoothness.

(III.ii.1)

This may appear to counter some of my arguments, but it shows
where the danger lay in Shakespeare's day: overmuch stress on
laboured and loud emphasis, and on elaborated gesture. We have an
insight into the style of acting favoured by contemporary
Shakespearian actors. Hamlet emphasises a toning-down, and, above
all, a delivery of tragic passion at once *torrential* and yet *temperate*.
It is not until we see that those are not opposites that we know the
truth of dramatic art. The actor should be above, and never subdued
by, his passion, which nevertheless remains intrinsic to what he is
doing.

It is a question of degree, so Hamlet continues:

Be not too tame neither, but let your own discretion be your tutor.
Suit the action to the word, the word to the action, with this
special observance that you o'erstep not the modesty of nature;
for anything so overdone is from the purpose of playing, whose
end, both at the first and now, was and is to hold, as 'twere,
the mirror up to nature. . .O, there be players that I have seen
play, and heard others praise, and that highly, not to speak it
profanely, that neither having the accent of Christians nor the
gait of Christian, pagan, nor man, have so strutted and bellowed
that I have thought some of nature's journeymen had made
men and not made them well, they imitated humanity so
abominably.

(III.ii.19)

That the action should correspond to the words, which may be
highly poetic, forces poetic gesture; but there is also, or at least
seems, a contradiction of my own and Barrault's contention that
there are times in the acting when you do not conform to normal
behaviour. All I can say is, that it is again a question of degree
and of what one is accustomed to see done. Hamlet, or Shakespeare,

had clearly seen some awful performances. Shakespeare's more
extravagant excursions must be interthreaded with realism and the
colloquial, must be carefully pinned to earth; and all should finally
seem, though not necessarily be, natural. Acting of any sort, as
well in prose farce as in high tragedy, should have a grace and a
harmony not found in normal behaviour. This is a subtlety Hamlet's
advice does not expressly survey.

What is most important in these speeches is the desire to find
in art a just balance of passion and temperance. Hamlet, as a man
apart from his poetry, does not show this. He finds in art what he
misses in life, except for Horatio, whom he, directly after his
speech to the Players, proceeds to address as follows:

> Since my dear soul was mistress of her choice
> And could of men distinguish, her election
> Hath seal'd thee for herself; for thou hast been
> As one, in suffering all, that suffers nothing,
> A man that fortune's buffets and rewards
> Hast ta'en with equal thanks; and bless'd are those
> Whose blood and judgment are so well co-mingled
> That they are not a pipe for fortune's finger
> To sound what stop she please. Give me that man
> That is not passion's slave, and I will wear him
> In my heart's core, ay, in my heart of heart,
> As I do thee.

                                                        (III.ii.68)

Observe that it is Hamlet's 'dear soul', his higher self, that requires the
qualities described. Horatio is regarded as a man who has come near to
attaining in life to the harmony of art. (Roy Walker, *The Time is out of
Joint*, 1948, p.71; also *The Wheel of Fire*, '*Hamlet* Reconsidered', 1949.)

There are thus two main impersonal concerns in *Hamlet*: death
and dramatic art. In what way can they be said to relate together?

In Hamlet's first soliloquy (I.ii.129-59) — a fine example of
suspended climax — suicide is considered desirable; in his last
(IV.iv.32-66), he admires Fortinbras' death-daring soldiership. In
between is the famous 'To be or not to be. . .':

> To be, or not to be: that is the question.
> Whether 'tis nobler in the mind to suffer

The slings and arrows of outrageous fortune,
Or to take arms against a sea of troubles,
And by opposing end them? To die: to sleep;
No more; and, by a sleep to say we end
The heart-ache and the thousand natural shocks
That flesh is heir to? 'Tis a consummation
Devoutly to be wish'd. To die, to sleep.
To sleep: perchance to dream. Ay, there's the rub;
For in that sleep of death what dreams may come
When we have shuffled off this mortal coil,
Must give us pause. There's the respect
That makes calamity of so long life;
For who would bear the whips and scorns of time,
The oppressor's wrong, the proud man's contumely,
The pangs of dispriz'd love, the law's delay,
The insolence of office, and the spurns
That patient merit of the unworthy takes,
When he himself might his quietus make
With a bare bodkin? Who would fardels bear,
To grunt and sweat under a weary life,
But that the dread of something after death,
The undiscover'd country from whose bourn
No traveller returns, puzzles the will,
And makes us rather bear those ills we have
Than fly to others that we know not of?
Thus conscience does make cowards of us all;
And thus the native hue of resolution
Is sicklied o'er with the pale cast of thought,
And enterprises of great pith and moment
With this regard their currents turn awry
And lose the name of action.

(III.i.56)

Though outwardly simple, the simplicity is deceptive. 'To be' refers
primarily neither to suicide nor to the act of revenge, though both may
be contained. It refers to a *state of being,* to realisation of one's total
self, which means the soul-self. This includes thoughts of suicide and
fine action ('enterprises of great pith and moment'), options which
are open to Hamlet but which he has not taken, perhaps, through,
as he says later, the fault

Of thinking too precisely on the event;
A thought which, quarter'd, hath but one part wisdom,
And ever three parts coward.

(IV.iv.41)

In this later soliloquy, on Fortinbras' heroic warring, he expressly
admires Fortinbras for his death-daring, as one who risks death and

Makes mouths at the invisible event,
Exposing what is mortal and unsure
To all that fortune, death and danger dare,
Even for an egg-shell.

(IV.iv.50)

The options of suicide and fine action are contained in Hamlet's 'To be
or not to be'; but he surveys them from above, and in doing so passes
in reverie beyond them. The nearest he gets to action is through the
play before the King, for which he has himself composed some lines.
His actions are often ill-judged, but his poetry is serene.

He is, like Richard II in prison, trying to adjust himself to his
own poetry; that is, to his own soul, for the language of the soul-self
is poetry. What Shakespeare means by the word 'soul' can be best
understood from a passage in *The Merchant of Venice* (V.i.58):

> Look, how the floor of heaven
Is thick inlaid with patines of bright gold.
There's not the smallest orb which thou behold'st
But in his motion like an angel sings,
Still quiring to the young-eye'd cherubins.
Such harmony is in immortal souls,
But whilst this muddy vesture of decay
Doth grossly close it in, we cannot hear it.

The soul is that in and beyond man that inspires his best moments on
earth and survives death. Shakespeare's use deserves study.

Such then is the meaning of 'To be or not to be' (see *The Wheel of
Fire*, '*Hamlet* Reconsidered', 1949). This search for the integral self is
likewise the key to Ibsen, in *Brand* and *Peer Gynt* (see my *Ibsen*, 1962).
Death is involved: Brand is at home with it and says: 'In Death I see
not overthrow' (V). Hamlet admires Fortinbras.

The realisation of the soul-self, the true poise of 'being', is one that exists fearlessly under the shadow, and on the brink, of death. Hamlet is not so much a tragic hero as a commentator on the tragic enigma. King Claudius is before him to be studied; Hamlet might also be said to use him in his play as a dramatic person. The King is sympathetically handled, as are all Shakespeare's tragic persons. His two long speeches, his advice to Hamlet against mourning overmuch (I.ii.87-117) and his wonderful prayer (III.iii.36-72), are especially notable. If it seems strange to regard him as almost a dramatic equal to Hamlet, we might consider that on the stage a superlative Hamlet would not be likely to be a good Othello, Macbeth, or Lear; but a superlative Claudius would be exactly right. He is the same kind of person as Shakespeare's future heroes.

However, Hamlet's story has a tragic rhythm of its own. He is originally a sensitive and good young man, but becomes more and more involved in evil, and acts dangerously. After his sea-adventure, he returns in a new mood. He is, we may say, drawing near to soul-realisation, and speaks accordingly. Though uneasy before the proposed duel, he accepts the situation and draws on the New Testament to speak of death with equanimity:

> *Horatio.* If your mind dislike any thing, obey it.
> I will forestall their repair hither, and say you are not fit.
> *Hamlet.* Not a whit. We defy augury. There's a special providence in the fall of a sparrow. If it be now, 'tis not to come; if it be not to come, it will be now; if it be not now, yet it will come. The readiness is all. Since no man has aught of what he leaves, what is't to leave betimes? Let be.
>
> (V.ii.229)

Hamlet is now at home with death. Because he has become thus integral, in the final scene revenge comes easily, almost as a subsidiary event, though at the cost of his own death. Horatio speaks his farewell:

> Now cracks a noble heart. Good night, sweet prince,
> And flights of angels sing thee to thy rest.
>
> (V.ii.373)

Alone among Shakespeare's heroes Hamlet is given this specific assurance.

I pass over the action of *Troilus and Cressida* (1601-2), where
Troilus has what may be called a tragic experience of great force, which
he surmounts. He is last seen on the battlefield as a blazing fury:

> I do not speak of flight, of fear, of death,
> But dare all imminence that gods and men
> Address their dangers in.

> (V.x.12)

He has tragic courage, but death is not involved.

Though the action avoids tragic form, we have at one point a
considered reading of tragic experience. The Greek leaders are discussing
their failure in war. Agamemnon argues that 'constancy' under Jove's
'trials' is a true test of manhood. Nestor expands this:

> In the reproof of chance
> Lies the true proof of men. The sea being smooth
> How many shallow bauble boats dare sail
> Upon her patient breast, making their way
> With those of nobler bulk!
> But let the ruffian Boreas once enrage
> The gentle Thetis, and anon behold
> The strong-ribb'd bark through liquid mountains cut,
> Bounding between the two moist elements
> Like Perseus' horse. Where's then the saucy boat
> Whose weak untimber'd sides but even now
> Co-rivall'd greatness? Either to harbour fled,
> Or made a toast for Neptune. Even so
> Doth valour's show and valour's worth divide
> In storms of fortune; for in her ray and brightness
> The herd hath more annoyance by the breese
> Than by the tiger; but when the splitting wind
> Makes flexible the knees of knotted oaks,
> And flies fled under shade, why then the thing of courage,
> As rous'd with rage, with rage doth sympathize,
> And with an accent tun'd in self-same key,
> Retorts to chiding fortune.

> (I.iii.33)

Exactly with such a defiance do Shakespeare's tragic heroes meet their destiny.

In *Measure for Measure* (1604), we have a close study of the moral
problem, concerned with men's unruly instincts and the inadequacy,
perhaps the impossibility, of legal control. The Duke's rule has been
accordingly lax. Angelo, a man of supposed rectitude, gives rein to
passion and thence to criminality, and is brought to repentance,
wishing for death; but the Duke too is, essentially, not all guiltless.
He is one who 'above all other strifes, contended especially to know
himself' (III.ii.252). This was presumably the reason for his lax rule:
he knew too well that there was sin in himself. If we put this beside
his extreme irritation at Lucio's account to him, when disguised as a
friar, about his supposed vices, we may suppose that he is recognising
an essential, though not an actual, truth (III.ii.125-72). Lucio's later
words, 'Nay, friar, I am a kind of burr; I shall stick' (IV.iii.193) drive
home such a reading. In the last scene the Duke finds it hardest of
all to forgive Lucio. The conclusion is enigmatic. If the Duke is, as
it seems, to marry Isabella, we have a conventional marriage used
to symbolise the union of tolerance and rectitude. Clearly, the play's
problem is related to our tragic heroes in whom passions are
unleashed, and who go to their end with self-recognition and
courage.

We have watched Shakespeare developing his tragic heroes in
dramas where their lonely importance is the less because of the
historic surrounds, and in *Romeo and Juliet* where there are two
leading persons of almost equal importance. In middle career, he
writes non-tragic dramas where a comedic and tragic person, Falstaff
and Shylock, obtrude powerfully, almost dangerously. In *Hamlet*
the problem is subtly examined from a number of angles. Now once
again, we ask, What is tragedy? Wherein lies what my brother called
'the tragic synthesis'? Shakespeare proceeds to give us a series of
great dramas where the tragic essence is isolated. Nietzsche in
The Birth of Tragedy saw Greek tragedy in terms of exultation
rather than failure; he may have been thinking as much, or more, of
Shakespeare as of the Greeks. The god of Greek tragedy was Dionysus,
a dangerous god. He is not a moral god; he is socially disruptive;
but he comes with great authority, and there is great purpose in
his revelation.

C.B. Purdom, in *What Happens in Shakespeare* (1963), writes:

What happens in tragedy is the defeat of the hero, and in defeat his regeneration, for it is of the nature of tragedy that the protagonist's destruction leads to his salvation, which is why tragedy is tolerable, even exhilarating. . . Thus the drama, through the reconciliation it establishes, is fulfilment in a new life: Dionysus torn to pieces but restored is the myth to which the drama is dedicated. (Part I, pp.27-8.)

George Steiner has an apposite comment:

It is a terrible, stark insight into human life. Yet in the very excess of his suffering lies man's claim to dignity. Powerless and broken, a blind beggar hounded out of the city, he assumes a new grandeur. Man is ennobled by the vengeful spite or injustice of the gods. It does not make him innocent, but it hallows him as if he had passed through flame. Hence there is in the final moments of great tragedy, whether Greek or Shakespearean or neo-classic, a fusion of grief and joy, of lament over the fall of man and of rejoicing in the resurrection of his spirit. No other poetic form achieves this mysterious effect; it makes of *Oedipus, King Lear,* and *Phèdre* the noblest yet wrought by the mind. (*The Death of Tragedy,* 1961; I, pp.9-10).

And here we may return to A.C. Bradley. His comments at the end of his discussion of *King Lear* are so important that I quote an extended passage:

. . . The feeling I mean is the impression that the heroic being, though in one sense and outwardly he has failed, is yet in another sense superior to the world in which he appears; is, in some way which we do not seek to define, untouched by the doom that overtakes him; and is rather set free from life than deprived of it. Some such feeling as this — some feeling which, from this description of it, may be recognised as their own even by those who would dissent from the description — we surely have in various degrees at the deaths of Hamlet and Othello and Lear, and of Antony and Cleopatra and Coriolanus. It accompanies the more prominent tragic impressions, and, regarded alone, could hardly be called tragic. For it seems to imply (though we are probably quite unconscious of the implication) an idea which, if developed, would transform the tragic view of things. It implies that the tragic world, if taken as it is presented, with all its error, guilt, failure, woe and waste, is no final reality, but only a part of reality taken for the whole, and when so taken, illusive; and that if we could see the whole, and the tragic facts in their true place in it, we should find them, not abolished, of course, but so transmuted that they had ceased to be strictly tragic — find, perhaps, the suffering and death counting for little or nothing, the greatness of the soul for much or all, and the heroic spirit, in spite of failure, nearer to the heart of things than the smaller, more circumspect, and perhaps even 'better' beings who survived the catastrophe. The feeling which I have tried to describe, as accompanying the more obvious tragic emotions at the deaths of heroes, corresponds with some such idea as this.

Now this feeling is evoked with a quite exceptional strength by the death of Cordelia. . . It is simply the feeling that what happens to such a being does not matter; all that matters is what she is. How this can be when, for anything the tragedy tells us, she has ceased to exist, we do not ask; but the tragedy itself makes us feel that somehow it is so. . . . . The more unmotived, unmerited, senseless, monstrous, her fate, the more do we feel that it does not concern her. The extremity of the disproportion between prosperity and goodness first shocks us, and then flashes on us the conviction that our whole attitude in asking or expecting that goodness should be prosperous is wrong; that, if only we could see things as they are, we should see that the outward is nothing and the inward is all.

Bradley has a footnote saying that he does not wish to complicate matters by the qualifications needed if he were to include the names of Macbeth and Lady Macbeth in his life of tragic heroes. I do not think that any exception should be made. He has another footnote saying that his tragic response must not be rendered explicit, or we should disturb the tragic impression. But why worry? We are under no obligation to feel miserable.

Too often producers and commentators, however clever they may be, show little awareness of what is happening. Perhaps I may be forgiven for quoting again, as I have before (in *Shakespearian Production*), these lines from *The Tempest*:

> *Antonio.* He misses not much.
> *Sebastian.* No. He doth but mistake the truth totally.
>
> (II.i.59)

The comment deserves a better context than that Shakespeare has given it.

5 THE FAMOUS TRAGEDIES

In *Othello* (1604) we have a protagonist of glamour. He is a Moor; and also, it would seem, a Christian. His appearance is variously discussed by commentators. Should he be an Arab or negroid? Aaron in *Titus Andronicus* was negroid, and phrases in the play suggest that Othello was too. That his rotund and richly-vowelled speech suggests Africa has been argued by Francis Berry in *Poetry and the Physical Voice*. I myself prefer, perhaps irrationally, to see his physiognomy as, in part at least, Semitic. However that may be, he has glamour from his adventures. He wins Desdemona by narrating them. He describes the manner of it:

> Her father lov'd me; oft invited me;
> Still question'd me the story of my life
> From year to year, the battles, sieges, fortunes
> That I have pass'd.
> I ran it through, even from my boyish days
> To the very moment that he bade me tell it;
> Wherein I spake of most disastrous chances,
> Of moving accidents by flood and field,
> Of hair-breadth 'scapes i' the imminent deadly breach,
> Of being taken by the insolent foe
> And sold to slavery; of my redemption thence,
> And portance in my travel's history;
> Wherein of antres vast and desarts idle,
> Rough quarries, rocks, and hills whose heads touch heaven,
> It was my hint to speak. Such was the process.
> And of the Cannibals that each other eat,
> The Anthropophagi, and men whose heads
> Do grow beneath their shoulders. This to hear
> Would Desdemona seriously incline;
> But still the house affairs would draw her thence;
> Which ever as she could with haste dispatch,
> She'd come again, and with a greedy ear
> Devour up my discourse.

(I.iii.128)

He tells how Desdemona asked for a full account; and the rest followed. Desdemona and Othello are married. Iago starts his plots, and Othello is distraught by jealousy.

Here we can see with peculiar clarity how exactly Shakespearian drama is poetically activated. Othello's way of speaking is ornate and its music noble: it is forecast by the opening of Morocco's speech in *The Merchant of Venice* (II.i.1):

> Mislike me not for my complexion,
> The shadow'd livery of the burnish'd sun.

This music Iago's plot would destroy.

The second half of a Shakespearian tragedy is usually preluded by some highly imaginative occurrence, lending it a new access of power. The occasion here is the loss of Desdemona's handkerchief. Not only does Othello suspect Desdemona of adultery, but he thinks she has parted with the magical handkerchief which he had given her; and it is not too much to say that this acts on his mind more powerfully than his other suspicion. Let us see what he says of it, what imaginative powers are generated:

> *Othello.* I have a salt and sorry rheum offends me.
> Lend me thy handkerchief.
>> *Desdemona.*   Here, my lord.
>> *Othello.* That which I gave you.
>> *Desdemona.*   I have it not about me.
>> *Othello.* Not?
>> *Desdemona.*   No, indeed, my lord.
>> *Othello.* That is a fault. That handkerchief
> Did an Egyptian to my mother give;
> She was a charmer, and could almost read
> The thoughts of people. She told her, while she kept it,
> 'Twould make her amiable and subdue my father
> Entirely to her love; but if she lost it,
> Or made a gift of it, my father's eye
> Should hold her loathèd, and his spirits should hunt
> After new fancies. She, dying, gave it me;
> And bid me, when my fate would have me wive,
> To give it her. I did so: and take heed on't;
> Make it a darling like your precious eye;

To lose't or give't away, were such perdition
As nothing else could match.
    Desdemona.   Is't possible?
    Othello. 'Tis true. There's magic in the web of it;
A sibyl that had number'd in the world
The sun to course two hundred compasses,
In her prophetic fury sew'd the work;
The worms were hallow'd that did breed the silk,
And it was dy'd in mummy which the skilful
Conserv'd of maidens' hearts.

(III.iv.52)

It is a truly wonderful 'Shakespearian inset' (I am thinking of Francis
Berry's admirable discussion of such excursions in his book *The
Shakespearian Inset,* 1965).

Othello's attack builds up with terrifying pressure: 'Is it lost?
is't gone? Speak, is it out o' the way?' When Desdemona denies
its loss Othello's accents become ominous: 'Fetch me the
handkerchief; my mind misgives.' He cries, and repeats it, 'The
handkerchief!' He storms out.

The power poetically generated here is pivotal. The drama's
activating impulse is in the realm of symbolism, poetically generated.
It is to be observed, as Middleton Murry pointed out ('Desdemona's
Handkerchief', *Shakespeare,* 1936, pp.312-13), that Desdemona
believes in the Handkerchief's power:

Sure, there's some wonder in this handkerchief;
I am most unhappy in the loss of it.

(III.iv.100)

That means, not, 'I must suppose from Othello's words that it is
remarkable and unique', but: 'I have just seen the powers of the
handkerchief in action.' Her emphasis could be: 'Sure, there *is* some
wonder. . .' The reading is supported by her 'Is't possible?' after
hearing Othello's description.

A handkerchief was in Shakespeare's 'source'; but it is what he
made of it poetically that is, as always, important. It was done by
the poetry, and the imaginative apprehension within the poetry.
But again, there is a truth behind it. As Lord Byron remarked,
'Shakespeare was right in making Othello's jealousy turn upon 'a

handkerchief, because 'the handkerchief is the strongest proof of love not only among the Moors, but all Eastern nations' (as reported by Thomas Medwin, *Conversations of Lord Byron,* 1824; and see Iris Origo, *The Last Attachment,* 1949; II, p.67 and note).

Subsequently Othello's anguish never for long forgets the handkerchief. He is made by Iago actually to see it in Cassio's hands; in his delirium he remembers it. Alexander Pope had the point in *'The Rape of the Lock':*

> Not fierce Othello in so loud a strain
> Roar'd for the handkerchief that caus'd his pain.
>
> (V.105)

In the final scene Othello, just before the murder, taxes Desdemona, not with adultery, but with giving away the handkerchief:

> *Othello.* That handkerchief which I so lov'd and gave thee
> Thou gav'st to Cassio.
>
> (V.ii.48)

She denies it. Again:

> *Othello.* By heaven, I saw my handkerchief in's hand.
> O perjur'd woman! thou dost stone my heart,
> And mak'st me call what I intend to do
> A murder, which I thought a sacrifice:
> I saw the handkerchief.
>
> (V.ii.62)

All this about the handkerchief, and only one minor suggestion ('That he hath us'd thee', V.ii.69) of adultery. Later, when defending himself, he refers to her having 'the act of shame a thousand times committed' (V.ii.209), but the very exaggeration reduces its importance, while he continues with the more detailed:

> And she did gratify his amorous works
> With that recognizance and pledge of love
> Which I first gave her. I saw it in his hand:
> It was a handkerchief, an antique token
> My father gave my mother.   (V.ii.211)

Othello had earlier said that it was given to his mother by an Egyptian 'charmer'. He here appears to be deliberately soft-pedalling the magic. Now the truth comes out; Emilia tells how she found it and gave it to Iago.

We can assume that Othello, as well as Desdemona, believes in the magical properties of the handkerchief and is hypnotised, after its loss, by a sense of magical domination. We might go yet further, and suppose that the magic is, up to a point, a real magic, and is responsible for Emilia's silence regarding the way it was lost; she too, is hypnotised by it. This would be hard for an actress to put across, though at the moment of final revelation there would be a fine opportunity, if the point were taken by the audience, to show her struggling to break free from the control, and succeeding. I think that we as an audience should, with a 'willing suspension of disbelief', accept the handkerchief's magical properties.

After Desdemona's death they do not, of course, exist: there is no need for them. Perhaps this is why Emilia is at last free to speak.

So much for this all-important poetic reality. In the later scenes, Othello, under the handkerchief's domination, plunges towards disaster. In the fourth act his utter disintegration is given disjointed prose:

> Lie with her! lie on her! We say, lie on her, when they belie her. Lie with her! that's fulsome. Handkerchief — confessions — handkerchief! To confess, and be hanged for his labour. First, to be hanged, and then to confess. I tremble at it. Nature would not invest herself in such shadowing passion without some instruction. It is not words that shake me thus. Pish! Noses, ears, and lips. Is it possible? — Confess! — Handkerchief! — O devil.
>
> (IV.i.35)

He falls in a fit unconscious. Nowhere can we see more clearly how, at an extreme, Shakespeare's use of a disjointed utterance is well conveyed by prose (though this is not to say that prose is not used often for serene purposes). There is much else of similar sort. Othello speaks to Desdemona like 'a beggar in his drink' (IV.ii.120).

Othello's story might be interpreted as a balance of poetry and prose; and, after a descent into prose of an extreme, disorientated sort, his poetry is magnificently recovered.

In the final scene he has regained his balance. He has voyaged through agony and loss of dignity to a new integrity and poise of being.

In this, his values are, I suppose, Oriental; they are not Christian. He is ploughing a lonely furrow, and it takes him into new worlds. He enters the bedroom. Desdemona is asleep. He addresses his own 'soul', his higher being, and all the splendours of his typical style are evident in this address:

> It is the cause, it is the cause, my soul.
> Let me not name it to you, you chaste stars!
> It is the cause. Yet I'll not shed her blood,
> Nor scar that whiter skin of hers than snow,
> And smooth as monumental alabaster.
> Yet she must die, else she'll betray more men.
> Put out the light, and then put out the light:
> If I quench thee, thou flaming minister,
> I can again thy former light restore,
> Should I repent me; but once put out thy light,
> Thou cunning'st pattern of excelling nature,
> I know not where is that Promethean heat
> That can thy light relume. When I have pluck'd the rose,
> I cannot give it vital growth again,
> It needs must wither: I'll smell it on the tree.
>
> *[Kisses Desdemona]*
>
> O balmy breath, that dost almost persuade
> Justice to break her sword! One more, one more.
> Be thus when thou art dead, and I will kill thee,
> And love thee after. One more, and this the last:
> So sweet was ne'er so fatal. I must weep,
> But they are cruel tears; this sorrow's heavenly,
> It strikes where it doth love.
>
> (V.ii.1)

'You chaste stars': he is voyaging into worlds unknown before. Othello is bent on a sacred duty. He is engaged not in a murder, but in a 'sacrifice' (V.ii.65). Patrick Cruttwell suggests that Othello's use of the concept may be compared with that of Brutus in *Julius Caesar* (II.i.166). The compulsion of this duty impinging on his love creates acute anguish, but he rises above it. The last lines reveal the opposites converging in his mind, and his transcending of them into a higher state: 'This sorrow's heavenly, it strikes where it doth love.' Heaven, or God, strikes down men while loving them; so Othello's experience is God-like.

There is more cosmic reference, directly following the murder. The poetry becomes incandescent:

> My wife! my wife! what wife? I have no wife:
> O, insupportable! O heavy hour!
> Methinks it should be now a huge eclipse
> Of sun and moon, and that the affrighted globe
> Should yawn at alteration.
>
> (V.ii.96)

This is followed soon after by:

> It is the very error of the moon;
> She comes more near the earth than she was wont,
> And makes men mad.
>
> (V.ii.107)

And then:

> Nay, had she been true,
> If Heaven would make me such another world
> Of one entire and perfect chrysolite,
> I'd not have sold her for it.
>
> (V.ii.141)

It does not matter that these images are sad; their impact is the greater for that. Othello sees the earth rather like a modern astronaut, as a great jewel swimming in space. These vast cosmic images of star, sun, moon and earth cluster close around the murder of Desdemona. At the moment when he first decided on his fearful but sacred course, Othello had enlisted the cosmic powers in his cause. Having determined on action, he concluded:

> Now, by yond marble heaven,
> In the due reverence of a sacred vow
> I here engage my words.

'Sacred vow': the compulsion was, to Othello, religious and Iago took up the hint with:

> Do not rise yet.
> Witness, you ever-burning lights above!
> You elements that clip us round about!
> Witness, that here Iago doth give up
> The execution of his wit, hands, heart,
> To wrong'd Othello's service!

(III.iii.461-8)

Imagistically, the cosmos and Othello act in unison.

In the final scene, after his recent disintegration, Othello emerges speaking in terms of a cosmic travel far beyond his early account of earthly adventure. Cosmic images cluster around the actual murder, and are as reflections of his travelling, and travailing, soul.

Before, we heard of his being sold to slavery and of his travels among cannibals and dwarfs, among sub-human kinds. Then followed his marriage and descent to near-insanity; then towering up, the prize of agony lived through and contained, this greater cosmic voyage of his soul among the planetary spaces. This he attains through *the coalescence of opposites,* love and the killing of love in response to a sacred duty: 'This sorrow's heavenly.' Here is his tragic synthesis and triumph, a pinnacle of near superhuman experience, his finest hour.

This will not be recognised without attention to the poetry; we need, as actors, to act the experience behind the poetry whilst speaking it. What, if any, gestures are in place must be left to the actor; facial expression, the eyes especially, will do much. For myself, I recall that I used a wide gesture for 'one entire and perfect chrysolite', limning out a great circle with my arms in definition, the eyes simultaneously expressing joy and wonder. Though this may appear excessive in print, it was not so in performance, not even noticeable within the total dramatic situation, where it appeared natural. Such gestures should, on occasion, grow out of a performance that is living the poetry, in small or great ways, moment by moment. I think that for poetic gestures the stage rule that gesture should precede speech may need reconsideration. It should accompany, sometimes even follow, the thought, to illustrate it, as part of what might be called a 'poetic naturalism'. After having registered the poetic reality, I changed to another style at 'I'd not have sold her for it', changing the facial expression and falling back on the colloquial, deliberately dropping away from the poetic, in order simultaneously to outline the poetry and pin it firmly to ordinary life. That is the method we should aim at.

These are the high moments in Othello's last scene. I do not rate as equally important Othello's crying out, when he realises his error, for damnation:

> Whip me, ye devils,
> From the possession of this heavenly sight!
> Blow me about in winds! roast me in sulphur!
> Wash me in steep-down gulfs of liquid fire!
> O Desdemona! Desdemona! Dead!
> Oh! Oh! Oh!
>
> (V.ii.276)

For one thing, one can hardly call this the finest poetry. It is what is demanded by the situation, and offered as a plot-necessity; no more. It is what Othello naturally feels, and should no doubt feel, but we who watch glory none the less in his error; we have *enjoyed* his tragedy, and its result in lonely, transcendental experience, and we accept the play's perfunctory conclusion for what it is worth. Of course, it is foolish to talk of Othello being actually damned. That is not stated (as it is in Marlowe's *Doctor Faustus*); also, theologically speaking, no one is less likely to go to Hell than he who demands it as his just deserts.

Again, his final speech, which is so often praised, does not seem to me more than a quiet ending, the aeroplane – as always in Shakespeare – coming to ground: the play has to be rounded off and the action framed by a return to normality. In it Othello returns to the manner and subject of his early travelogue, concerned, as Francis Berry observed after hearing the recital on which these pages are based, with earthly adventures. As in his cry for damnation, he is again, it seems, a Christian – though Hell comes in Moslem beliefs too – reporting how he killed a 'circumcised' Turk for opposing the Venetian state. His killing himself may be un-Christian. It is to be regarded according to heroic, un-Christian, valuations: 'This did I fear', says Cassio, 'for he was great of heart' (V.ii.359).

What I am here concerned to observe is Othello's rise, through tragedy, to a pinnacle of lonely experience and luminous poetry, just before and after the murder, with poetic ratification of a high order.

Our next play, *Macbeth* (about 1606), presents difficulties, since it so
obviously counters our moral judgements. If *Titus Andronicus* forecasts
King Lear, Richard III even more exactly forecasts *Macbeth*. Macbeth
is at the start a man of action. His fighting has been excessively bloody
and is so described. He is a brave soldier, praised by everyone, including
King Duncan, who loads him with honours. Soon after we first meet
him he is shown in a peculiarly nervous state. He has heard the
prophecies of the Weird Sisters and is deeply disturbed, shaken to the
depths of his being. He meditates:

> Two truths are told,
> As happy prologues to the swelling act
> Of the imperial theme. I thank you, gentlemen.

After this brief aside to those who have brought the news, he returns —
it is a characteristic of his — to meditation:

> This supernatural soliciting
> Cannot be ill, cannot be good; if ill,
> Why hath it given me earnest of success,
> Commencing in a truth? I am Thane of Cawdor.
> If good, why do I yield to that suggestion
> Whose horrid image doth unfix my hair
> And make my seated heart knock at my ribs,
> Against the use of nature? Present fears
> Are less than horrible imaginings.
> My thought, whose murder yet is but fantastical,
> Shakes so my single state of man that function
> Is smother'd in surmise, and nothing is
> But what is not.

(I.iii.127)

The speech is jerky, nervy, expressing a state near to nervous disorder.
Banquo says, 'Look, how our partner's rapt.' He is, pretty nearly,
'rapt' like this for the greater part of his drama.

Before the murder he is fearful, and almost decides against it. We
have a remarkable soliloquy that starts in nervous spasms, but develops
into a grand flow of poetry holding superlative images: a fine example
of the normal Shakespearian build-up from colloquial realism to
poetic sublimity, such as we found in Henry IV's sleep-speech. We

start with heavily impeded phrases:

> If it were done when 'tis done, then 'twere well
> It were done quickly; if the assassination
> Could trammel up the consequence, and catch
> With his surcease success; that but this blow
> Might be the be-all and the end-all here,
> But here, upon this bank and shoal of time,
> We'd jump the life to come.

The verse is ugly and constricted; the sibilants hold us up; it is awkward to speak, and comes from a mind in distraction. When Shakespeare wants a congested and ugly verse to express a state of unease he knows how to do it. The voice should reflect this. It advances to a smoother and more rational manner:

> But in these cases
> We still have judgement here; that we but teach
> Bloody instructions, which being taught, return
> To plague the inventor; this even-handed justice
> Commends the ingredients of our poison'd chalice
> To our own lips.

The issues are being, hesitatingly, clarified and soon become yet clearer:

> He's here in double trust:
> First, as I am his kinsman and his subject,
> Strong both against the deed; then as his host,
> Who should against his murderer shut the door,
> Not bear the knife myself.

The poetry grows now stronger, with powerful imagery:

> Besides, this Duncan
> Hath borne his faculties so meek, hath been
> So clear in his great office, that his virtues
> Will plead like angels trumpet-tongu'd against
> The deep damnation of his taking-off;
> And pity, like a naked new-born babe,

Striding the blast, or heaven's cherubin, hors'd
Upon the sightless couriers of the air,
Shall blow the horrid deed in every eye,
That tears shall drown the wind.

After that, spoken with attention to nothing but the poetry – no
nervous disorder in the voice – we return to earth, and a colloquial
utterance, summing up the whole:

I have no spur
To prick the sides of my intent, but only
Vaulting ambition, which o'erleaps itself
And falls on the other.

(I.vii.1-28)

We have no finer example of poetic build-up, rising from a disjointed
start. It is as a commentary on the whole drama; but yet not
exactly that. For observe: it is a moral statement. Shakespeare has
a sterner task in hand: to elicit our sympathy and even admiration
for a man guilty of appalling crimes. To this task his powers are
next devoted.

His wife rouses him by appealing to his bravery, and Macbeth
engages himself to the murder almost from fear of fear. In his
address to the 'air-drawn' dagger he is at once agitated and purposeful,
and with a supreme effort banishes it from his sight. This is our
first example of his courage in face of the supernatural. Then:

Thou sure and firm-set earth,
Hear not my steps, which way they walk, for fear
Thy very stones prate of my whereabout,
And take the present horror from the time,
Which now suits with it.

(II.i.56)

He is perfectly aware of the true nature of his crime, and has
already condemned himself; but he accepts, and willingly
embraces, the 'present horror'; he has aligned himself with
it, we do not know why. As A.C. Bradley noted, he undertakes

the murder as an 'appalling duty'.*

After the murder, he is again unsettled, and fearful. He has murdered sleep itself:

> Methought I heard a voice cry 'Sleep no more!
> Macbeth does murder sleep', the innocent sleep,
> Sleep that knits up the ravell'd sleave of care,
> The death of each day's life, sore labour's bath,
> Balm of hurt minds, great nature's second course,
> Chief nourisher in life's feast.

(II.ii.36)

He is struck with terror at the knocking on the gate:

> How is't with me, when every noise appals me?
> What hands are here? Ha! they pluck out mine eyes.
> Will all great Neptune's ocean wash this blood
> Clean from my hand? No, this my hand will rather
> The multitudinous seas incarnadine,
> Making the green one red.

(II.ii.59)

He knows what he has done and recognises the appalling nature of his guilt. On the discovery of the murder, he pretends innocence, and yet strangely, as though it were his higher self, or soul, that were speaking, he tells what is the very truth of his own destiny:

> Had I but died an hour before this chance
> I had liv'd a blessed time; for, from this instant,
> There's nothing serious in mortality.
> All is but toys; renown and grace is dead,
> The wine of life is drawn, and the mere lees
> Is left this vault to brag of.

(II.iii.8)

---

*In his introduction to his drama *Gregory VII*, R.H. Horne observed: 'Whatever the crime, there is always something grand and solemn in exploring the depths of human nature. The wisest or the shallowest sitter-in-judgment would tremble and be mute were the criminal's thoughts and passions all laid bare to view. In the worst acts, it is probable, we might find within the individual something exculpatory, if not redeeming; something which, *under the circumstances, seemed right*; something, at heart, the very opposite to his one fatal act.' (*Gregory VII*, 1840; p.xvi.)

As Middleton Murry has observed (*Shakespeare,* 1936, p.332) Macbeth knows, or half-knows, or his soul knows, that this is the turning point, for himself; and he is later brought to full knowledge of it. He has killed the King's guards, pretending to suspect them, but, while his action is hateful, his words on Duncan in death ring true:

> Here lay Duncan,
> His silver skin lac'd with his golden blood;
> And his gash'd stabs look'd like a breach in nature
> For ruin's wasteful entrance. . .

(II.iii.118)

He can clothe his deception in such finery, which is there, in part, for our, the audience's reception; but there is a genuine feeling in it, which must be vocalised. Macbeth is for the moment outside himself and his deed, contemplating it with pity. Throughout he is aware of such implications. Again, it is his 'soul' that speaks.

Macbeth has, pretty nearly, sold himself to uttermost evil. But the strange thing is that he is, in a way, empowered by it.* Being now King, he has a new dignity, like Richard III. His first soliloquy as King is in a more resonant and full-blooded style than those that preceded. In the second half royalistic images hold poetic authority. We may say that he speaks with the royal voice of a Claudius rather than the spiritualised voice of a Hamlet. There is the usual build-up:

> To be thus is nothing;
> But to be safely thus. Our fears in Banquo
> Stick deep, and in his royalty of nature
> Reigns that which would be fear'd: 'tis much he dares,
> And, to that dauntless temper of his mind,
> He hath a wisdom that doth guide his valour

---

*Compare John Marston, *Antonio's Revenge,* III.v., where the previously gentle Antonio, having tasted blood, addresses his Father's ghost:

> Methinks I am all air and feel no weight
> Of human dirt clog. This is Julio's blood!
> Rich music, father: this is Julio's blood!

See also Edward Young's *Busiris, King of Egypt* for a peculiarly neat correspondence to the fortuitous course of events in *Macbeth,* as if the gods designed it (III). These plays are handled in my *The Golden Labyrinth,* pp.98, 193.

> To act in safety. There is none but he
> Whose being I do fear; and under him
> My genius is rebuk'd, as it is said
> Mark Antony's was by Caesar. He chid the sisters
> When first they put the name of king upon me,
> And bade them speak to him. Then, prophet-like,
> They hail'd him father to a line of kings.
> Upon my head they plac'd a fruitless crown,
> And put a barren sceptre in my gripe,
> Thence to be wrench'd with an unlineal hand,
> No son of mine succeeding. If't be so,
> For Banquo's issue have I fil'd my mind;
> For them the gracious Duncan have I murder'd;
> Put rancours in the vessel of my peace
> Only for them; and mine eternal jewel
> Given to the common enemy of man,
> To make them kings, the seed of Banquo kings!
> Rather than so, come fate into the list,
> And champion me to the utterance!

(III.i.48)

He fixes on Banquo, as a tangible fear. There is also a recognition that his own kingship is uncreative, whereas Banquo's descendants are to enjoy future sovereignty. The poetry of kingship rolls out with great assurance: it is what Macbeth has murdered Duncan for, and craves for, but as yet without full enjoyment. He thinks that his 'eternal jewel', or soul, has incurred damnation for it, and ends with a challenge to Fate itself. His lonely self is embattled against Fate. He knows, in one sense, that it is a losing battle, but his course is set. The poetry neverthless has a new assurance.

Macbeth may be said to develop throughout the theme of conscience which comes in *Richard III* only at the end. It is a play about conscience, very largely, and labours to establish in drawn-out action the victory over conscience which was briefly compacted in the earlier work. He would crush his conscience even at the cost of wholesale destruction:

> But let the frame of things disjoint, both the worlds suffer,
> Ere we will eat our meal in fear, and sleep
> In the affliction of these terrible dreams,

That shake us nightly. Better be with the dead,
Whom we, to gain our peace, have sent to peace,
Than on the torture of the mind to lie
In restless ecstasy. Duncan is in his grave;
After life's fitful fever he sleeps well.
Treason has done his worst: nor steel, nor poison,
Malice domestic, foreign levy, nothing
Can touch him further.

(III.ii.16)

Conscience is active in sleep, but he tries courageously to adjust
himself to evil:

Ere the bat hath flown
His cloister'd flight, ere, to black Hecate's summons
The shard-borne beetle with his drowsy hums
Hath rung night's yawning peal, there shall be done
A deed of dreadful note.

(III.ii.40)

He brushes aside Lady Macbeth's query 'What's to be done?' with
'Be innocent of the knowledge dearest chuck, till thou applaud the
deed', and characteristically — I say 'characteristically', since the
play is largely soliloquy — returns to his own brooding thoughts:

Come, seeling night,
Scarf up the tender eye of pitiful day,
And with thy bloody and invisible hand
Cancel and tear to pieces that great bond
Which keeps me pale! Light thickens, and the crow
Makes wing to the rooky wood;
Good things of day begin to droop and drowse,
Whiles night's black agents to their preys do rouse.

(III.ii.46)

'Pitiful' shows that he is well aware of the softer valuations; the 'great
bond' of the compulsion on man to goodness keeps him 'pale'. His
'soul' is again speaking to him. Nevertheless he embraces the
darkness.

In *Macbeth*, it is difficult to quote anything without quoting

everything. The play is very largely a monologue. Macbeth tends to
address a few words to his interlocutor, and then return to the
inwardness of poetic meditation. It is one long soliloquy, far more than
Hamlet, where the soliloquies are so closely involved with externals that
they have an objective quality: he is talking about the world outside, as
Macbeth is not.

We now come to the Banquet scene. Macbeth has heard of Banquo's
murder, which has been carried out under his direction. He now formally
expresses regret at Banquo's absence from the feast; and at this moment
the Ghost appears, either, like the air-drawn dagger, as a figment of his
own conscience, or as an actuality. Probably the former, as no one else
sees it. Macbeth is utterly at a loss. His words reflect as much:

> Prithee, see there! behold! look! lo! how say you?
> Why, what care I? If thou canst nod, speak too.
> If charnel-houses and our graves must send
> Those that we bury back, our monuments
> Shall be the maws of kites.
>
> (III.iv.69)

It starts with a sequence of interjections, and the remainder is
undistinguished, almost inapposite. The Ghost disappears. Macbeth
meditates on past terrible murders:

> Blood hath been shed ere now, i' the olden time,
> Ere human statute purg'd the general weal;
> Ay, and since too, murders have been perform'd
> Too terrible for the ear. The times have been
> That, when the brains were out, the man would die,
> And there an end. . .
>
> (III.iv.75)

He speaks as though he were not a murderer himself, preserving full
recognition of the horror of murder in a civilised community. He is
regarding himself, perhaps rightly, as basically a good man, shocked:
one part of him, his soul, *is* shocked. He then recovers himself and
with extreme courage deliberately, as it were, as Granville-Barker has
noted (*Prefaces,* VI, p.76),* *dares* the Ghost to return:

*For Macbeth's courage before the Ghost of Banquo, see also Willard Farnham,
Shakespeare's Tragic Frontier (as below), II, pp.122-5.

> Come, love and health to all!
> I drink to the general joy of the whole table,
> And to our dear friend Banquo, whom we miss;
> Would he were here! To all, and him, we thirst,
> And all to all.

(III.iv.87)

It reappears, perhaps in a different position, where least expected: on the throne perhaps. But now Macbeth summons up a new courage. His contest has been all the time with intangible realities, and his victory here is notable as a victory over the intangible, or supernatural:

> Avaunt! and quit my sight! Let the earth hide thee!
> Thy bones are marrowless, thy blood is cold;
> Thou hast no speculation in those eyes
> Which thou dost glare with.

(III.iv.93)

That is, it is not fully human, not even a real ghost, but a subjective fabrication. The actor's voice should express scorn. Again:

> What man dare, I dare:
> Approach thou like the rugged Russian bear,
> The arm'd rhinoceros, or the Hyrcan tiger;
> Take any shape but that, and my firm nerves
> Shall never tremble: or be alive again,
> And dare me to the desert with thy sword;
> If trembling I inhabit then, protest me
> The baby of a girl. Hence, horrible shadow!
> Unreal mockery, hence!

(III.iv.99)

The Ghost vanishes. We are to take it as a figment of Macbeth's conscience; as basically 'unreal', a 'mockery'. As with the air-drawn dagger before, Macbeth masters the apparation: we are invited to watch his courage in face of the horror. Physical courage, as the lines indicate, was his always; what the whole drama illustrates throughout is Macbeth's striving to mastery of a deeper fear, the infra-natural horrors of crime and evil. Our speech invites this interpretation, and we applaud Macbeth's courage. He wins, driving the phantom away.

From now onwards he is set on a lonely course:

> For mine own good
> All causes shall give way: I am in blood
> Stepp'd in so far, that, should I wade no more,
> Returning were as tedious as go o'er.

(III.iv.135)

He visits the Weird Sisters again. He addresses them as their superior. He
has, like Milton's Satan confronted by Death and Evil in *Paradise Lost,*
a human status (for Satan is humanly conceived) greater than theirs.
They are creatures of infra-human reality.

> *Macbeth.* How now, you secret, black and midnight hags!
> What is't you do?
>   *The Sisters.*   A deed without a name.

(IV.i.48)

Though infra-human, they have powers unknown to man, and to these
powers Macbeth subjects himself at the risk, or cost, of universal chaos:

> I conjure you, by that which you profess —
> Howe'er you come to know it — answer me:
> Though you untie the winds and let them fight
> Against the churches; though the yesty waves
> Confound and swallow navigation up;
> Though bladed corn be lodg'd and trees blown down;
> Though castles topple on their warders' heads;
> Though palaces and pyramids do slope
> Their heads to their foundations; though the treasure
> Of Nature's germens tumble all together,
> Even till destruction sicken; answer me
> To what I ask you.

(IV.i.50)

He does not compromise with his conscience, like King Claudius in
Hamlet; rather he knows that having once broken with good, he is
plunging towards a universal nihilism. What is perhaps most striking
in Macbeth's story is his extraordinary honesty throughout.

There follow the Apparitions, whose impact, contrasting destruction with creation, I have often discussed. To their import Macbeth is blind, listening to their words only, unaware of their visual impact. He demands to know if Banquo's descendants will reign, and is shown a procession of them, future kings, passing to Music, in contrast to the Apparitions who came to Thunder. We may observe that, like the Handkerchief scene in *Othello,* an incident of a highly imaginative order is, in Shakespeare's usual manner, the agent of the drama's advance, unleashing new life.

Macbeth has been told to beware of Macduff, and now decides to surprise his castle and murder his wife and family. His descent is rapid. We have a scene showing the surprise, and the murders. With Macduff and Malcolm in England we hear of the horrible slaughter: Ross comes from Scotland to report the chaos it is in. Fixing Macduff with his eye, he says:

> Your eye in Scotland
> Would create soldiers, make our women fight,
> To doff their dire distresses.

(IV.iii.186)

'Create' for Macduff's children, 'women' for his wife: it is a way of breaking the news, which now follows, in all its horror. Then:

> *Malcolm.* Be this the whetstone of your sword: let grief
> Convert to anger; blunt not the heart, enrage it.
> *Macduff.* O! I could play the woman with mine eyes,
> And braggart with my tongue. But, gentle heavens,
> Cut short all intermission; front to front
> Bring thou this fiend of Scotland and myself;
> Within my sword's length set him; if he 'scape,
> Heaven forgive him too!

(IV.iii.227)

The scene is easy to receive and applaud: it says what we, as a normal audience, want said. Audiences will applaud strongly, with a greater enthusiasm probably than they have showed hitherto. All our human and moral valuations are engaged.

One might wonder what Shakespeare is up to. His usual way of maintaining sympathy with his protagonist seems at this point to be absent. What we should note, however, is what he is up *against*. Without shirking one jot of criminality, his drama is, or will be, at pains to accomplish, as near as may be, its usual task.

For directly after this we move to Lady Macbeth's Sleep-walking scene. After we have witnessed the extremity of Macbeth's criminality in the report of Lady Macduff's and her child's murder, the more hideous when we watch the reaction of those who receive the news; just after this, we are within Lady Macbeth's room, with her gentlewoman and the Doctor, and hear Lady Macbeth's prose mutterings in sleep. She is in a kind of Hell: 'Hell is murky' (V.i.39). Then:

> Here's the smell of the blood still: all the perfumes of
> Arabia will not sweeten this little hand.
>
> (V.i.55)

Strangely, paradoxically, almost unfairly, Macduff's rhetoric, still sounding in our ears, is like tinkling cymbals in comparison with these prose jettings from the depths. It is an extreme example of Shakespeare's countering of poetic afflatus with colloquial − yet here so much more than that − idiom. It corresponds to those other scenes of fourth-act calm, usually accompanied by music, that recur throughout Shakespeare's tragedies. It acts on us like music.

Wherein lies the especial wonder of this scene? Perhaps it is Lady Macbeth's soul that speaks, as from a new dimension, aware of her crime, reminding her of it; that 'soul' in us that has prompted Macbeth's remembrance, throughout his story, of the good which he is opposing. There is somewhere contained in this scene all the mystery of evil; for evil is innately mysterious, as good is not. Shelley, in his *Defence of Poetry,* has an apt passage:

> Even crime is disarmed of half its horror and all its contagion
> by being represented as the fatal consequence of the unfathomable
> agencies of nature; error is thus divested of its wilfulness; men can
> no longer cherish it as the creation of their choice. In a drama of the
> highest order there is little food for censure or hatred; it teaches
> rather self-knowledge and self-respect.

We can scarcely improve on that. Perhaps Shelley was thinking of this scene. The Doctor speaks the only adequate comment:

> Unnatural deeds
> Do breed unnatural troubles; infected minds
> To their deaf pillows will discharge their secrets;
> More needs she the divine than the physician.
> God, God forgive us all!

(V.i.78)

There is no condemnation. We may compare the not dissimilar delirium of the guilt-stricken Cardinal Beaufort in *2 Henry VI,* and the King's comment, 'Forbear to judge, for we are sinners all' (III.iii.31).

In the battle scenes we are in a new world. In 'On the Ghosts in the Tragedies of Shakespeare' Edward Gordon Craig writes: 'In the last act Macbeth awakes. It almost seems to be a new role. Instead of a sleep-walker dragging his feet heavily he becomes an ordinary man startled from a dream to find the dream true' (*On the Art of the Theatre,* edition of 1957, p.269). John Masefield writes: 'Let him not play the later scenes like a hangman who has taken to drink, but like an angel who has fallen' (*A Macbeth Production,* 1945, p.31). From mystery and darkness we climb to the mountain's height, beyond and above the murk. Macbeth is fearless. At last, the call is for physical courage, and that comes easily. Macbeth and his opposers share equally in this daylight activity dispelling nightmare. He is avid for his armour:

> *Macbeth.* I'll fight till from my bones my flesh be hack'd.
> Give me my armour.
> *Seyton.*   'Tis not needed yet.
> *Macbeth.* I'll put it on.
> Send out more horses, skirr the country round;
> Hang those that talk of fear. Give me mine armour.

(V.iii.32)

Macbeth should be performed in these scenes as a figure rejuvenated by the challenge of action; and action in an honest cause, because he knows, and others know, that he is a criminal fighting for his life. He is no longer afraid of the infranatural horrors:

> I have almost forgot the taste of fears.
> The time has been my senses would have cool'd
> To hear a night-shriek, and my fell of hair
> Would at a dismal treatise rouse and stir

As life were in't. I have supp'd full with horrors;
Direness, familiar to my slaughterous thoughts,
Cannot once start me.

(V.v.9)

Earlier he had said:

I am in blood
Stepp'd in so far, that, should I wade no more,
Returning were as tedious as go o'er.

(III.iv.136)

He has elected to go 'o'er', and succeeded. He is now, on every level,
bold, because honest.

A personal reminiscence may here be in place, of how the actor may
be empowered by the poetic action to an unsuspected strength. I played
Macbeth in a production by Brownlow Card in 1939. In rehearsal I was
given a weighty weapon, iron, with a ball and spikes at the end, to
carry in the war-scenes. I said it was too heavy. I could hardly lift it,
and wanted at first to do without it, though I eventually submitted. At
one point Macbeth was to run *up* steps, shouting:

Ring the alarum bell! Blow, wind! come, wrack!
At least we'll die with harness on our back.

(V.v.51)

Whilst running, I waved and waggled the deadly weapon above my head.
My mind, for an instant, stepped outside of my performance to notice
that it was, at that instant, *light as a feather.* The poetry of the occasion,
the drama, had either dissolved it, or made me ten times stronger. Such
is the power that may be generated, how I do not know. Perhaps
adrenalin had something to do with it.

Countering the action of these last scenes, we have three superb
pieces of poetry, of a more inward sort. They are probably the best
pieces of poetry that Macbeth has to offer; and that indeed says much.
At last his main poetic vice – if so we can call it – of talking only,
though in superb poetry, of what concerns himself, is gone; at least
the three pieces I shall now quote are all of universal interest. As
with Richard II and Romeo – and Lear – he moves toward the
impersonal. Our first is about age:

> This push
> Will cheer me ever or disseat me now.
> I have liv'd long enough: my way of life
> Is fall'n into the sear, the yellow leaf;
> And that which should accompany old age,
> As honour, love, obedience, troops of friends,
> I must not look to have; but in their stead,
> Curses, not loud but deep, mouth-honour, breath,
> Which the poor heart would fain deny, and dare not.

(V.iii.20)

This is spoken gravely, but not brokenly. Macbeth's integrity is firm, and never more so than when, as here, he sees and admits truth. There is nothing 'confessional' in it; he is determined still on his course; but there is recognition. He has always been aware, far more so than other Shakespearian heroes, of the issues involved; he is a sinner aware of, and in part subscribing to, virtue. A strange blend, germane to his poetry throughout. He is in this way more to be praised than some of the less guilty heroes, for it is by self-knowledge that the Shakespearian hero is reclaimed. Richard III attained to it at the end, and all the rest, one after the other. Our clearest example occurs in *Henry VIII*, when Wolsey, who represents ambition, has been unmasked by the King:

> I know myself now, and I feel within me
> A peace above all earthly dignities,
> A still and quiet conscience. The King has cur'd me.

(III.ii.379)

He is 'cured', and attains religious peace, simply by being found out. This is not repentance; it is a new honesty with himself and his community, and an open relation at last, based on acceptance.*

After quoting Macbeth's 'I have liv'd long enough' speech, C.B. Purdom writes: 'What follows, the actor usually carries out as a defeated man, a criminal at bay, which is entirely wrong, for having faced his end Macbeth in the light of that acceptance is able to accept everything, his spirit rising ever higher as his fortunes fall'

---

*It corresponds to the New Testament *metanoeite,* if translated as 'change your life direction' rather than 'be sorry for your past sins'. This may be the true meaning of what is usually translated as 'repent'.

(*What Happens in Shakespeare,* Part III, p.158). Or, to put it rather
differently, Macbeth is unrepentant, but self-condemned.
   Our second speech is on the mental disorder of Lady Macbeth:

   Macbeth. How does your patient, doctor?
   Doctor.   Not so sick, my lord,
As she is troubled with thick-coming fancies,
That keep her from her rest.
   Macbeth.   Cure her of that:
Canst thou not minister to a mind diseas'd,
Pluck from the memory a rooted sorrow,
Raze out the written troubles of the brain,
And with some sweet oblivious antidote
Cleanse the stuff'd bosom of that perilous stuff
Which weighs upon the heart?
   Doctor.   Therein the patient
Must minister to himself.

(V.iii.37)

The whole realm of mental disorder is here surveyed, and a just
conclusion reached in the Doctor's words. The speech is one of
universal interest and application.
   Our third comes at Macbeth's reception of the news that Lady
Macbeth is dead:

She should have died hereafter;
There would have been a time for such a word.
To-morrow, and to-morrow, and to-morrow,
Creeps in this petty pace from day to day,
To the last syllable of recorded time;
And all our yesterdays have lighted fools
The way to dusty death. Out, out, brief candle!
Life's but a walking shadow, a poor player
That struts and frets his hour upon the stage,
And then is heard no more; it is a tale
Told by an idiot, full of sound and fury,
Signifying nothing.

(V.v.17)

That is a final statement of a possible reading of life and death; or put better, it records what is undeniably part of our apprehension. It is a truth we ought to face before we go further. It is spoken proudly. If one speaks it brokenly, as from a man in despair, one contradicts the poetry, and a just performance becomes impossible. That is why Macbeth is so often considered a difficult part; the actor approaches it in a manner that is at odds with the poetry. The first lines are spoken with all the majesty due to the grand survey. At 'Out, out, brief candle!' Macbeth rejects life and its trivial concerns with a gesture of proud dismissal; not, at all costs, sad, but mighty in its rise above all human dealings. In performance I now, rather boldly, use gestures at the end, hands up and eyes wild for 'idiot', and then crushing back on the closed eyes for 'nothing'. Macbeth has reached a state-of-being beyond, or above, time; and the rest is unknown, or undefined.

That this speech has been compared by Middleton Murry in a fine essay 'The Nature of Poetry' (*Discoveries,* 1924) with Prospero's 'Cloud-capp'd towers' speech (*The Tempest,* IV.i.148-58) argues its semi-mystic properties. Murry even regarded it as too good for Macbeth:

> There speaks a despair beyond Macbeth's; it comes like a moan of wild and superhuman music into the play, a divine visitation. It is a despair beyond Macbeth's, for it is not the despair of crime, but of mortality; not of a murderer, but a victim; and it could have come even more truly from the greatest and noblest spirit in the world.

Therefore, says Murry, we have reason to regard it as Shakespeare's own, personal, comment; but our reading of Shakespeare's tragedies shows that it is perfectly in order, since Shakespeare is in the habit of developing his tragic heroes until they speak, as it were, beyond themselves. If the speech were not convincing there might be reason to complain; but it is convincing, since Macbeth has throughout spoken marvellous lines and at the conclusion is doing better than ever. Nothing could more firmly support my reading of Shakespeare's tragic methods than Murry's unwillingness to regard this crucial speech as Macbeth's.*

What we can, undisputably, say is, that in his last scenes Macbeth speaks three speeches of generalised import, speeches that can be quoted

---

*I should record that in his subsequent *Shakespeare* (1936, pp.334-6), Middleton Murry regards the speech as suited to its context. John Lawlor in *The Tragic Sense in Shakespeare* (1960, pp.137-41), devotes an extended discusssion to the lines, which he regards as of central importance. See also Roy Walker *The Time is Free,* 1949, pp.190-4.

by us all for our usual affairs without respect to his story, though they
are perfectly in place in that story: one on old age, another on mental
disturbance, and the third on life's futilities. I was thinking of these
speeches when in my 1923 final examination at Oxford I wrote:
'Shakespeare is greatest not when he is differentiating character from
character, but when his people give expression to thoughts of
universal application' (or something close to that). Such is the glory
won by Macbeth as a poetic person; for it is the poetry which we are
considering.

How this reading relates to morality, I do not presume to know
with any certainty. Moral values are preserved, though a schoolboy
I once taught wished that they were not, and that Macbeth had killed
Macduff. At the last, Macbeth thinks that he may do so and his
conscience again, as so often before, is awakened:

> Of all men else I have avoided thee:
> But get thee back, my soul is too much charg'd
> With blood of thine already.
>
> (V.vii.33)

He actually wants Macduff, his worst enemy, to live on. He cannot
however well avoid the fight. Asked to surrender, he replies:

> I will not yield,
> To kiss the ground before young Malcolm's feet,
> And to be baited with the rabble's curse.
> Though Birnam wood be come to Dunsinane,
> And thou oppos'd, being of no woman born,
> Yet I will try the last: before my body
> I throw my warlike shield. Lay on, Macduff,
> And damn'd be him that first cries, 'Hold, enough!'
>
> (V.vii.56)

He knows and admits that he has merited 'the rabble's curse'. The
prophecies from the Weird Sisters have deluded him. He is thrown
back on himself and on his courage. The final values of Shakespearian
tragedy are the heroic values: that is why, though Macbeth earlier
in the play expected damnation, now at the end, he relates damnation
to lack of courage. This is deeply Shakespearian.

We may go some way towards relating the play to our normal

thought by observing that both here and in *Hamlet* supernatural figures
are seen first by everyone, and half-way through by the hero alone
(I am thinking of Lennox' denial of having seen the Weird Sisters after
the Cauldron scene); and finally they do not exist for us, since it
would be quite inapposite to have the Ghost in *Hamlet* or the Weird
Sisters in *Macbeth* appear — it has been done — in the last scenes.
From which we can perhaps deduce that there are unrestful forces
abroad and that the hero takes on himself to express them, and
thereby dissolve the evil. I do not say that we have any clear reason
for supposing this, but it is a possible way of making sense of our
enigma.*

Edward Gordon Craig (page 96 above) saw Macbeth and Lady
Macbeth as hypnotised by 'unseen agencies' until the final act. If this
be so, we can say that his moments of moral recognition fight against
the hypnotism, until the horror is dispelled.

Morality is, as elsewhere, outwardly preserved. Macbeth is given no
stately end, and his head appears, affixed to a pole. The framework is
there, as always; but it would be an error to confuse the frame with
the picture. The picture has riveted our attention, from scene to
scene; and it has been largely a picture of Macbeth's poetry; indeed
more personally so than is usual, since the drama is so much of a
monologue. With consummate realism Shakespeare refuses to point
to anything like this, but he does better. In the last speech, Malcolm
refers to 'this dead butcher and his fiend-like queen' (V.vii.98), and
is amply justified in doing so. The effect on us, however, who have
been far more interested in the real poetry than the fictional events,
is exactly the opposite. Our natural response is, 'Yes, but —'. We are
aware of the depths and heights we have enjoyed, through the very
adventures of these two, and their desperate battling with, perhaps
through, the dark powers. When Macbeth refuses to kiss the ground
before young Malcolm's feet, we may recall Richard III's contemptuous
dismissal of 'shallow Richmond' (page 27 above); and we remember too
the Weird Sisters' words spoken early, as a kind of prologue:

> Though his bark cannot be lost
> Yet it shall be tempest-tost.   (I.iii.24)

---

*This reading of the drama has been developed in my *Christ and Nietzsche*, 1948
(III, pp.85-6); and in *Shakespeare and Religion*, pp.188-92. The reading may be said
to have some authority from Ulysses' 'Order' speech in *Troilus and Cressida*,
where evils on earth are said to be caused by planetary divagation (I.iii.94-5),
man's disruptive actions being to this extent forced.

It could not have been better put. Nowhere can we see more clearly
how it is in the nature of dramatic poetry to survey the total
situation. Macbeth is always supremely aware of what he is doing, and
what it means. At the end he is more than ever aware, and dies with
a co-presence of guilt and integrity.

I conclude with George Steiner's admirable words on such heroes,
'But they stride to their fierce disasters in the grip of truths more
intense than knowledge' (*The Death of Tragedy,* I, p.7).

King Lear (about 1606, perhaps preceding *Macbeth*) shows some
striking exploitations of tragic advance. In the early scenes Lear is a
variously tyrannic and pathetic figure, demanding of the actor a fair
amount of 'character' acting as a petulant old man.

He finds himself rejected by his two elder daughters. He is fearful
in his wrath. He is also pathetic. When the elder daughters together
confront him, we have a poignant moment:

> Who comes here? O heavens,
> If you do love old men, if your sweet sway
> Allow obedience, if yourselves are old,
> Make it your cause; send down and take my part!

(II.iv.192)

Lear's variations are interesting, if not always attractive:

> I prithee, daughter, do not make me mad.
> I will not trouble thee, my child; farewell.
> We'll no more meet, no more see one another;
> But yet thou art my flesh, my blood, my daughter;
> Or rather a disease that's in my flesh,
> Which I must needs call mine. Thou art a boil,
> A plague-sore, an embossèd carbuncle,
> In my corrupted blood. But I'll not chide thee.
> Let shame come when it will, I do not call it:
> I do not bid the thunder-bearer shoot,
> Nor tell tales of thee to high-judging Jove.
> Mend when thou canst; be better at thy leisure.
> I can be patient; I can stay with Regan,
> I and my hundred knights.

(II.iv.221)

The old man's voice is very evident in those last four lines.

Lear's agony is long drawn out, as he moves from one daughter to the other, and finds himself, in effect, turned down by both. His cause is summed up, and given a new strength, in a long, and crucial, transition speech:

> But, for true need —
> You heavens, give me that patience, patience I need!
> You see me here, you gods, a poor old man,
> As full of grief as age; wretched in both!
> If it be you that stir these daughters' hearts
> Against their father, fool me not so much
> To bear it tamely; touch me with noble anger,
> And let not women's weapons, water-drops,
> Stain my man's cheeks! No, you unnatural hags,
> I will have such revenges on you both
> That all the world shall — I will do such things —
> What they are yet I know not — but they shall be
> The terrors of the earth. You think I'll weep;
> No, I'll not weep.
> I have full cause of weeping, but this heart
> Shall break into a hundred thousand flaws
> Or ere I'll weep. O fool! I shall go mad.

(II.iv.273)

He goes out, with the Fool, on to the storm-riven heath. This speech is central, registering first pathos and then anger, and finally courage and the embracing of tragic agony, even to madness. Lear has hitherto been petulant, absurdly irascible, weak by turns. Now he asserts his integrity. 'No, I'll not weep' is the pivot.

When we next see him, he has a new stature. The drama enjoys a new and different lease of life. We enter a new world, and a new type of acting is demanded. No longer do we think primarily of an old man. Hardly any suggestion of age is wanted now, as it has been before, in the voice; not at first anyway. Instead, we think only of the poetic extravaganza, and how to convey it, by voice and gesture.

Lear speaks, turned right (left side to the audience), and addresses the storm off-stage. The setting is craggy, and Lear raised. There is slashing rain, lightning, and thunder, in that order. Intermittent rolls

of thunder curve up above the speaking voice, which falls and remains
silent till they have passed. There should be no simultaneous conflict
of sounds, but an intermittence. The actor's right hand is out, pointed
at the storm. At 'cataracts' it points up. At 'thought-executing fires'
the hand zig-zags rapidly, living them; and then comes back, drawn
across the forehead, turned towards the audience, at 'singe my white
head'. Thunder comes just before it is mentioned. Here is the speech:

> Blow, winds, and crack your cheeks! rage! blow!
> You cataracts and hurricanoes, spout
> Till you have drench'd our steeples, drown'd the cocks!
> You sulphurous and thought-executing fires,
> Vaunt-couriers to oak-cleaving thunderbolts,
> Singe my white head! And thou, all-shaking thunder,
> Strike flat the thick rotundity o' the world!
> Crack nature's moulds, all germens spill at once
> That make ingrateful man!
>
> (III.ii.1)

The Fool speaks, and then Lear, again, after a loud burst of thunder,
stronger than before, though the speech ever so slightly falls back into
self-pity, and ends colloquially:

> Rumble they bellyful! Spit, fire! spout, rain!
> Nor rain, wind, thunder, fire, are my daughters.
> I tax not you, you elements, with unkindness;
> I never gave you kingdom, call'd you children,
> You owe me no subscription. Then, let fall
> Your horrible pleasure; here I stand, your slave,
> A poor, infirm, weak and despis'd old man.
> But yet I call you servile ministers,
> That have with two pernicious daughters join'd
> Your high-engender'd battles 'gainst a head
> So old and white as this. O! O! 'Tis foul.
>
> (III.ii.14)

Towards the end age will again be apparent in the voice, spoken quietly,
followed soon after by 'No, I will be the pattern of all patience. I will
say nothing' (III.ii.37). But the titanic rise has been generated.

The thunder should be shatteringly loud. I am reminded of

Beerbohm Tree, who, when he complained that the thunder at a
rehearsal was inadequate and was told that it was not stage thunder
but that a real storm was raging outside, replied: 'Well, it may satisfy
the people outside, but we must do better at His Majesty's.' Tree's wit,
at its best, tended – far more than Wilde's – to act in depth.

Next, Lear becomes more self-less, sensing divine justice
over-arching human wickedness:

> Let the great gods,
> That keep this dreadful pother o'er our heads,
> Find out their enemies now. Tremble, thou wretch,
> That hast within thee undivulgèd crimes
> Unwhipp'd of justice. Hide thee, thou bloody hand;
> Thou perjur'd and thou simular of virtue
> That art incestuous; caitiff, to pieces shake,
> That under covert and convenient seeming
> Hast practis'd on man's life. Close pent-up guilts,
> Rive your concealing continents, and cry
> These dreadful summoners grace. I am a man
> More sinn'd against than sinning.

(III.ii.49)

At 'close pent-up guilts', the hands are low and cupped together; at
'rive' they are torn violently apart; and are ready to be raised high
for 'grace'. Such actions live the poetry, and drive it home over the
whole theatre. They have the additional merit of making clear the
meanings of 'pent-up', 'rive' and 'continents', which are strange to
the modern ear; but this is only a peculiarly emphatic example of
what such gestures always do in living the words and making them
transfix.

We only want this sort of action occasionally, but should be
ready for it, all stops out, when needed. Directly after, Lear talks
colloquially, with age in the voice:

> My wits begin to turn.
> Come on, my boy. How dost, my boy? Art cold?
> I am cold myself. Where is this straw, my fellow?

(III.ii.67)

And then comes a further advance in selflessness:

> Poor naked wretches, whereso'er you are,
> That bide the pelting of this pitiless storm,
> How shall your houseless heads and unfed sides,
> Your loop'd and window'd raggedness, defend you
> From seasons such as these? O! I have ta'en
> Too little care of this. Take physic, pomp;
> Expose thyself to feel what wretches feel,
> That thou mayst shake the superflux to them,
> And show the heavens more just.
>
> (III.iv.28)

This is a prelude to the appearance of Edgar, disguised as Tom
O'Bedlam.

From now on there is a new dimension in the phantasmagoria, led
by naked Tom (page 134 below). Lear descends into madness, which
is a mixture of prose inconsequence and poetic profundity. Here it
will be enough to point to the profundity, which concentrates
mainly on sex:

> When I do stare, see how the subject quakes.
> I pardon that man's life. What was thy cause?
> Adultery?
> Thou shalt not die: die for adultery! No:
> The wren goes to't, and the small gilded fly
> Does lecher in my sight.
>
> (IV.vi.111)

The 'gilded fly' recalls *Titus Andronicus* (page 22 above). Lear
continues:

> Let copulation thrive; for Gloucester's bastard son
> Was kinder to his father than my daughters
> Got 'tween the lawful sheets.
> To't luxury, pell-mell! for I lack soldiers.
> Behold yond simpering dame, .
> Whose face between her forks presageth snow,
> That minces virtue, and does shake the head
> To hear of pleasure's name.
> The fitchew nor the soilèd horse goes to't
> With a more riotous appetite.

> Down from the waist they are centaurs,
> Though women all above;
> But to the girdle do the gods inherit,
> Beneath is all the fiends'.
> There's hell, there's darkness, there is the sulphurous pit,
> Burning, scalding, stench, consumption. Fie, fie, fie!
> Pah, pah! Give me an ounce of civet, good apothecary, to sweeten
>   my imagination.
>
> (IV.vi.117)

Some of this may appear 'out of character'; but what we should see is,
that it is the aim of Shakespearian tragedy to get its hero, through
suffering, to a state of being wherein a generalised view of the human
situation is unveiled. Satire may be involved:

> Thou rascal beadle, hold thy bloody hand!
> Why dost thou lash that whore? Strip thine own back.
> Thou hotly lust'st to use her in that kind
> For which thou whip'st her. The usurer hangs the cozener.
> Through tatter'd clothes small vices do appear,
> Robes and furr'd gowns hide all. Plate sin with gold,
> And the strong lance of justice hurtless breaks;
> Arm it in rags, a pygmy's straw does pierce it.
>
> (IV.vi.165)

In and through his madness Lear searches out truths unknown to his
sanity. Every scene notches out an advance.

His madness is given a pictorial, summery description:

> Alack! 'tis he. Why, he was met even now
> As mad as the vex'd sea, singing aloud;
> Crown'd with rank fumiter and furrow weeds,
> With burdocks, hemlock, nettles, cuckoo-flowers,
> Darnel, and all the idle weeds that grow
> In our sustaining corn.
>
> (IV.iv.1)

This is spoken by Cordelia. His reunion with her, his loving daughter
whom he had rejected, gives us an intensely moving scene. Lear
has slept, and is recovering. Music sounds. He wakes:

> *Lear.* You do me wrong to take me out o' the grave.
> Thou art a soul in bliss, but I am bound
> Upon a wheel of fire, that mine own tears
> Do scald like molten lead.
>> *Cordelia.*   Sir, do you know me?
> *Lear.* You are a spirit I know. When did you die?
>
> (IV.vii.45)

This reunion, with Lear's final recovery, in its realisation of love, and love's humility, is shot through with semi-transcendental meaning. Nothing can destroy its beauty, its power, and its serenity.

After the battle, Lear and Cordelia are prisoners. In his new-found love that does not matter. He is above all earthly concerns.

> *Lear.*   Come, let's away to prison.
> We two alone will sing like birds i' the cage.
> When thou dost ask me blessing, I'll kneel down,
> And ask of thee forgiveness. So we'll live,
> And pray, and sing, and tell old tales, and laugh
> At gilded butterflies, and hear poor rogues
> Talk of court news. And we'll talk with them too,
> Who loses and who wins, who's in, who's out,
> And take upon's the mystery of things,
> As if we were God's spies; and we'll wear out,
> In a wall'd prison, packs and sets of great ones,
> That ebb and flow by the moon.
>
> (V.iii.8)

Lear is in a state-of-being that enjoys an eternal recognition from which the ambitions and rivalries of mankind are — as they were to Romeo — transcended; have become almost laughable; but there is much more than that. He sees through events into their 'mysteries', and expects to outspace and outlive the comings and goings, 'ebb and flow', of humanity, as from a higher, eternal consciousness. The lines are spoken as from second childhood, according to Powys a state of wisdom (*Letters to Nicholas Ross*, Arthur Uphill (ed.), 1971, pp.137-40, 146, 154). Babies weep because they know all life is folly (IV.vi.187-8). The word 'God' is important; *King Lear* has advanced from the paganism of its early and middle action to the medieval ritual of the combat between Edgar and Edmund (see my 'Tragedies of Love' in *Books and Bookmen,* Vol.16, No.5, February 1971); ending with 'God's spies'. Once again, a notch is registered in Lear's advance. He has attained a God-like consciousness.

Then comes the tragic climax. Cordelia is hanged, and Lear distraught. This marks, in one sense, a fall, but it is a fall in the usual Shakespearian fashion, after poetic height and descent, the aeroplane coming to earth. It is an extreme example of Shakespeare's way of giving a colloquial, or otherwise normal, ending after sublimity. Even so, Lear's courage and strength is emphasised:

> *Lear.* I kill'd the slave that was a-hanging thee.
> *Officer.* 'Tis true, my lord, he did.
> *Lear.*   Did I not, fellow?
> I have seen the day, with my good biting falchion
> I would have made them skip. I am old now,
> And these same crosses spoil me.
>
> (V.iii.276)

The end is simultaneously poignant and ambiguous. Lear speaks ('fool' is a term of endearment, for Cordelia):

> And my poor fool is hang'd! No, no, no life!
> Why should a dog, a horse, a rat, have life,
> And thou no breath at all? Thou'lt come no more,
> Never, never, never, never, never!
> Pray you, undo this button: thank you, sir.
> Do you see this? Look on her, look, her lips.
> Look there, look there!
>
> (V.iii.307)

We have a powerful instance of the usual interplay in Shakespeare of the colloquial against passion, in 'undo this button'. After that, Lear thinks Cordelia alive. He had placed a feather on her lips before, and apparently thinks she is breathing. Then comes the enigmatic, 'Look there, look there!' He may see, or think that he sees, her form, in the new life before him: it is quite usual for people nearing death to see their dead relatives. He had already been aware of her as 'a soul in bliss' (page 109). Lear dies. Kent speaks:

> Vex not his ghost. O let him pass; he hates him

That would upon the rack of this tough world
Stretch him out longer.

(V.iii.314)

This seems to assert belief in the after-life. The 'ghost', or 'spirit', is to
be allowed to 'pass', or it will be angry. Kent expects for himself
a continuity of existence:

I have a journey, sir, shortly to go.
My master calls me. I must not say no.

(V.iii.323)

We today too easily dismiss, or are oblivious to, such all-important
details.*

What we have to observe in *King Lear* is the hero's steady advance,
in descent from *Titus Andronicus,* step by step, in his pilgrimage. The
effects are easy to understand: from a tyrannic and petulant old man
to poetic sublimity in his address to the storm, to sympathy with
impoverished humanity, to the profound insights of his madness; to
the reunion with Cordelia, and his speech of 'eternal' recognition.
These must be accepted, without clouding them by knowledge of
the sad end. Lear and Cordelia would have had to die eventually,
anyway: it is always what happens within the drama that is important,
not the ending, except to note that the drama is shadowed by death,
for which the rest is a preparation.

King Lear is a comparatively simple play to treat within our present
purpose, because the advance is naturally aligned with our moral
approval. As Sadhan Kumar Ghosh observes (in his book, *Tragedy,*
Calcutta, 1965), Lear is the only tragic-hero in Shakespeare who repents;
it is a repentance, however, not before God, but before a human being,
Cordelia.

In these three tragedies, *Othello, Macbeth* and *King Lear,*
Shakespeare has concentrated as never before on the tragic essence,
and in so doing has developed his stories to a unification of his heroes
with their own poetic selves, or souls. I am reminded of Charles

---

*See also my article 'Gloucester's Leap', *Essays in Criticism* (July 1972;
   Vol.XXII, No.3), wherein I suggest possible deeper implications in
   Gloucester's mock-suicide.

Purdom's contention in *What Happens in Shakespeare* (1963): that poetic tragedy is to be taken as an autobiographical record by the protagonist, envisioned by him at the moment of death: 'It is not a going back into history, repeating what then took place. . .but the re-experiencing of the events not as the past or as the present but in the timelessness of consummation. In this timeless view the hero is delivered from the ego-centricity of time, he escapes from the prison of his ego. Thus it is of the very essence of the dramatic hero that his ego has been transformed in the course of the action. . .the world of the play is wholly within the vision of the protagonist' (p.28).* There may well be something like this going on, at least with these three plays, if not elsewhere. They are highly spiritualised works celebrating the protagonist's errors, poetic achievement, and triumph. To give this achievement a just expression is the dramatic challenge of which I write. So often our performances show no recognition whatsoever of what is happening.

*A BBC dialogue between Purdom and myself discussing his theory is recorded in my *Shakespeare and Religion*, 1967.

6 TIMON OF ATHENS

We shall now discuss *Timon of Athens* (?1608-9), which raises a
number of difficult questions; so many, indeed, that I here depart from
my usual method of discussing the work of art in and for itself only
and leaving questions of the artist's life and 'intentions' out of it.
Where a work of art is satisfactory and coherent, that will be our aim;
but *Timon of Athens* is not a perfected work of art. Parts of it read
rather like an unfinished, or unrevised, text, laid aside for
reconsideration. True, I have hitherto treated it as complete, being
engaged on a pure interpretation, and that only (much the same applies
to *Macbeth,* which looks like a cut version). For a change, if for no
other reason, I will here adopt a less astringent approach.

   Timon of Athens sums up Shakespeare's tragic sequence. However
inspired Shakespeare may have been, he must presumably have had
some knowledge of what he had been doing. He will have seen that he
had been creating a number of persons gigantic in their poetic power,
who were yet, outwardly, ordinary men in conflict with their
environment. He had, in fact, been creating half-fledged supermen,
what we may call 'dramatic' supermen, who outwardly fail in their
contest but are inwardly victorious; bloody but unbowed. In the process
vast forces are unleashed: in *Othello,* the magical Handkerchief; in
Macbeth occult powers; in *King Lear* the violent tempest, and mad
Tom. These are forces of cosmic threat and disruption which swirl
around the hero but are not exactly located in him; as though he has
unleashed forces that henceforward control the events. These forces
may be called, in Nietzsche's sense, 'Dionysian'. At the conclusion
sanity and morality are restored, and the 'dramatic superman' is gone.

   What did this mean? What did it mean to Shakespeare? I will
hazard some guesses. I think he was aware of the challenge of
these protagonists, though he did not know precisely who or what
they were. He had been conscious of the tragic enigma, and in his
middle period been aware of the embarrassment of Falstaff and
Shylock in their respective contexts. He had turned it all over in
Hamlet, and came to the conclusion that the aim of man was the
achievement of a state of being, not too easily defined. He had then
written the great tragedies in search of definition; but he is still

unsatisfied. Realism had been so inflated, almost too inflated, by the poetry. Othello was in one sense a rough soldier, 'rude' in speech (I.iii.81), but in another, an instrument of superb poetry. Which was the truth? The only person in Shakespeare where tragic power was closely assimilated to realism came in a comedy: Shylock.* This problem is naturally aligned with moral questions. The hero is immoral, and yet glorified. Is that finally satisfactory? Perhaps it is, the way Shakespeare did it, but he himself may have been disturbed. What, then, to do next? He has created 'dramatic supermen'; but what of a real superman? can he do that?

He decides to compose a play which has no such discrepancies; a play with a hero who has on every level a near-superman status, and who so incorporates the drama in himself that no external Dionysian effects, no external magic or tempests, are needed to accompany the tragic reversal. The powers of other dramas unleashed across the world are here to be contained in the hero as a person. Like others, he will be, in essence, a lonely person, at least in his tragic experience; but the poetic achievement touched by others will be by him fully *possessed.* He will be in himself a person of magical radiations corresponding to the magic of the poetry spoken by earlier heroes; and he will be sought after by his community, as a saviour. His tragic advance will not be intermittent, as in *King Lear,* nor a matter of last-act sublimity, as in *Othello,* but will be deliberate, controlled and expanded. What those earlier heroes attained briefly, Timon will enjoy with full purpose over an extended period. In this way Shakespeare aims to write a tragedy interpreting and surpassing all previous tragedies; what we may call an 'archetypal' tragedy.

The first half of *Timon of Athens* is admirably planned and constructed. Scenes of great skill and dramatic force succeed each other with a pleasing inevitability. It is almost too good, as though very carefully deliberated. The Poet's description of his poem serves as a prologue:

> I have in this rough work shap'd out a man
> Whom this beneath world doth embrace and hug
> With amplest entertainment. My free drift
> Halts not particularly, but moves itself

---

*For my complete study of Shylock, see *Shakespearian Production* (1964).

In a wide sea of wax: no levell'd malice
Infects one comma in the course I hold,
But flies an eagle flight bold and forth on
Leaving no tract behind.

(I.i.44)

'Shap'd out a man'; the deliberate attempt to *fabricate* a hero
is suggested. These first scenes are all 'fabricated', though with extreme
assurance and skill. 'Halts not particularly' means 'is not limited by
particularity'; is instead universal.

But problems arise. His hero is to end as a Promethean figure,
severed from his community, and exerting near-magical powers. So
much is clear. But how to get him there? He must be, so far as possible,
without fault. Shakespeare creates, accordingly, an ideal man. To
Shakespeare, in his Renaissance way of thought, this meant a great
and benevolent Lord. He seizes on what little there is to be told of
Timon in Plutarch's *Antonius*. The name 'Timon' is apposite,
suggesting 'worth' and 'honour'. So he creates Timon, who becomes a
Renaissance prince, benevolent and rich, patron of the arts, but also
anxious to help anyone of lower status, arranging the marriage of his
servant with financial assistance and paying a friend's debts;
entertaining his friends and loading them with gifts and receiving gifts
in return; with feasts, dances, including a Masque of the Five Senses,
and in general a grand display of Renaissance culture, sensuously and
ardently conceived. Politically, he is the prototype of a benevolent
and unselfish aristocracy, saying 'I myself would have no power'
(I.ii.36).

It is wrong to see Timon's friends as gross flatterers. In the Feast
scene, which should, with its masque and dance, be presented as a
riot of *controlled* sensuousness, they are a company of people
enjoying themselves mightily, respectful to Timon, but no more. They
give and take presents. Apemantus may call them insincere, but
they are not that, while things go well. We all know that it is easy
to be convivial with friends in the same income group as ourselves,
but when one falls from equality, and becomes a would-be borrower,
or in some other way a suitor, things assume a different aspect. These
and the subsequent scenes are levelled at all of us, and in them we
recognise, or should recognise, an embarrassing truth.

This is, though archetypal, a very 'personal' work, and it would seem
that Shakespeare is relying on his own personal experience. In the

Sonnets Shakespeare celebrates his adoration of a young man of quality, and its gradual expansion, as I have shown in *The Mutual Flame,* to a more universal love; that universal love is exactly what beats within Timon's unlimited benevolence. It is noteworthy, as I have argued in 'New Light on the Sonnets' in my *Shakespeare and Religion,* that *Timon of Athens* was probably composed about the time that the Sonnets (which may date from earlier, though they may have been often revised) were published; that is, in 1609. Timon's universal benevolence may not be quite convincing; it is rather like the white of an egg with the yolk still to come. The two parts correspond to Elizabethan idealism (with Timon matching Theseus in *A Midsummer Night's Dream*) and Jacobean revulsion; or in Nietzsche's terms, Apollonian and Dionysian.

The severance from his community has to be manipulated, and that means that there must be something abnormal in Timon's behaviour, corresponding to what was wrong, or 'immoral', in earlier heroes. The main problem in these plays is to get the hero *alone,* for only in his loneliness is the next stage of being advanced. Timon's fault is his almost unbelievable generosity,* and his money is soon exhausted. He is guilty not of a sin, but of folly, and that, in a way, reduces his dignity, since we respond to a crime with more admiration than we give to foolishness. But there is more to be said. We are probably wrong in so doing; and Shakespeare at least has pointed our sympathies by uncompromising choric passages of first importance, directed against his erstwhile friends who will not help him in his financial straits:

> *First Stranger.* Why this is the world's soul; and just of the same
>   piece
> Is every flatterer's spirit. Who can call him
> His friend that dips in the same dish? For, in
> My knowing, Timon has been this lord's father,
> And kept his credit with his purse,
> Supported his estate. Nay, Timon's money
> Has paid his men their wages; he ne'er drinks
> But Timon's silver treads upon his lip.

---

*That it is not really so unbelievable may be gathered from my study *Jackson Knight: a Biography* (Alden Press, Oxford, 1975). See p.476 and index.

And yet, O see the monstrousness of man
When he looks out in an ungrateful shape,
He does deny him, in respect of his,
What charitable men afford to beggars.
    Third Stranger. Religion groans at it.
    First Stranger.   For mine own part,
I never tasted Timon in my life,
Nor came any of his bounties over me,
To mark me for his friend. Yet I protest,
For his right noble mind, illustrious virtue,
And honourable carriage,
Had his necessity made use of me,
I would have put my wealth into donation,
And the best half should have return'd to him,
So much I love his heart.

                                  (III.ii.72)

Shakespeare knows that there is a danger of our not responding to
Timon's nobility, and does all he can, here and elsewhere, to build up
his hero with passages of 'choric' comment. That is partly what I mean
by calling these scenes 'fabricated'; and yet, dramatically, there is no
real failure.

    'When he looks out in an ungrateful shape'. We are pointed above all
to ingratitude. Here Shakespeare is playing on a favourite theme,
almost an obsession: ingratitude. We get it in *Twelfth Night,* in
Antonio's embittered words to the boy Sebastian, whom he loved
and had befriended:

    Antonio.   Will you deny me now?
Is't possible that my deserts to you
Can lack persuasion? Do not tempt my misery,
Lest that it make me so unsound a man
As to upbraid you with those kindnesses
That I have done for you.

                                  (III.iv.383)

He is mistaking Viola for her twin brother, and Viola replies:

    Viola.   I know of none.
Nor know I you by voice or any feature.

I hate ingratitude more in a man
Than lying, vainness, babbling, drunkenness,
Or any taint of vice whose strong corruption
Inhabits our frail blood.

(III.iv.388)

Ingratitude aligns itself naturally with false friends. As early as
The Two Gentlemen of Verona we have:

Thou common friend, that's without faith or love —
For such is a friend now — treach'rous man!
Thou has beguil'd my hopes: nought but mine eye
Could have persuaded me. Now I dare not say
I have one friend alive: thou wouldst disprove me.
Who should be trusted now, when one's right hand
Is perjur'd to the bosom?

(V.iv.62)

In *As You Like It* the song 'Under the greenwood tree' is emphatic:

Blow, blow thou winter wind,
Thou art not so unkind
          As man's ingratitude. . .

and

Freeze, freeze, thou bitter sky,
Thou dost not bite so nigh
          As benefits forgot. . .

and

Most friendship is feigning, most loving mere folly. . .

(II.vii.174)

Or again as late as Buckingham's farewell in *Henry VIII:*

Where you are liberal of your loves and counsels,
Be sure you be not loose; for those you make friends
And give your hearts to, when they once perceive

The least rub in your fortunes, fall away
Like water from ye, never found again
But where they mean to sink ye.

(II.i.126)

Ingratitude is a powerful element in *King Lear,* where Lear's madness
turns largely on a sense of 'ingrateful man' (III.ii.9). Again:

Filial ingratitude!
Is it not as this mouth should tear this hand
For lifting food to 't?

(III.iv.14)

It is 'thou marble-hearted friend' (I.iv.283).

In *Julius Caesar* both Pompey and Caesar endure a communal
'ingratitude' (I.i.59; III.ii.190). In *Titus Andronicus* Tamora warns
Saturninus to move carefully:

Lest then the people, and patricians too,
Upon a just survey, take Titus' part,
And so supplant you for ingratitude,
Which Rome reputes to be a heinous sin. . .

(I.i.445)

Rome's ingratitude is emphasised. A Goth addresses Titus' son, Lucius:

Brave slip, sprung from the great Andronicus,
Whose name was once our terror, now our comfort,
Whose high exploits and honourable deeds
Ingrateful Rome requites with foul contempt,
Be bold in us.

(V.i.9)

So, too, is Athens guilty of ingratitude to Timon:

Forgetting thy great deeds, when neighbour states,
But for thy sword and fortune, trod upon them. . .

(IV.iii.94)

Timon is honoured for his past services to the state, and experiences

ingratitude. He takes on Andronicus' mantle: a strange coming-together
of Shakespeare's first sombre tragedy and his last.

In *Timon of Athens* Shakespeare is on ground well known to
him, and his most cherished valuations appear to be engaged.
Timon's tragedy 'is not that he is reduced to poverty and cast off,
but that the godlike image of man in his heart is cast down, and
his dreams of human fellowship destroyed' (Peter Alexander,
Shakespeare's Life and Art, 1939, p.184). This is pre-eminently
Shakespeare's personal statement, used for his most generalised
tragic adventure. Stripped to its essence, he gives us tragedy
unadorned and rendered explicit.

The action pivots on the second Feast, to which Timon invites
those who have refused to help him. He pretends to be friendly, and
next speaks a speech of withering sarcasm, and upsets the Feast.
I see him as overturning the table or tables, with a crash of crockery,
and driving all before him with his staff, like Christ and the
money-dealers in the Temple. Then, after a long diatribe of universal
denunciation, he casts off his robes:

> Nothing I'll bear from thee
> But nakedness, thou detestable town!
> Take thou that too, with multiplying bans!
> Timon will to the woods, where he shall find
> The unkindest beast more kinder than mankind.

(IV.i.32)

He leaves Athens for the wilds.

The change is abrupt, and Timon's long curses that follow
may seem insufficiently motivated. The move from personal
disillusionment to wholesale condemnation may appear too extreme;
but that is what happens. Ingratitude may have seemed to Shakespeare
a sufficient motive, but a difficulty remains. There is nothing new
in his attack, nothing he could not have known before. What
has happened is that his view of man has just been tilted towards
negations. 'Ingratitude' was the supposed cause, but if we do
not think that sufficient, we can imagine something else.

The long curses do not build up and flower out in Shakespeare's usual manner, but exist on one level.* Though violent, they read as statements of material already in Shakespeare's mind rather than as discoveries during composition. The same is true of *Troilus and Cressida,* which likewise reads as a drama of personal statement: Shakespeare appears to have gone to Greek stories on such occasions, as in *Pericles* too.† The second half of *Timon of Athens* is in one sense as 'fabricated' as the first; but instead of the emotions and fine climax of that, we have a settled deployment of material that might be called 'static', though the wisdom contained is so impressive that criticism is inept. Shakespeare has now got Timon where he wants him, and he becomes a voice for a poetry ranging widely over human and natural existence, stripping it bare and facing the predicament of ignoble man in a majestic but hard universe.

A Shakespearian tragedy, as I have repeatedly emphasised, regularly shows an unleashing of new power about half-way through. Here the principle is driven to an extreme, with a new pattern of action supervening; rather as in *King Lear,* only more structurally simple.

We now find Timon in the wilds, addressing the sun. For the setting, I favour a suggestion of trees in the foreground ('Timon will to the woods') and a rocky coastline upstage, with the sea heard beyond. Timon wears only a rough loin-cloth, a little longer one side than the other, so that it can fall significantly. He is by the rocks, his naked figure first silhouetted in darkness, but gradually gilded and thrown up by the rising sun:

> O blessed breeding sun! Draw from the earth
> Rotten humidity; below thy sister's orb
> Infect the air!

(IV.iii.1)

---

*We may have to assist the writing with our own artistry. The succession of curses in IV.i, if spoken at high pressure throughout, would be almost impossible for the actor and unbearable for the listener. If it is spoken in full, the actor does best to start quietly, as though breathless from recent actions; or pensively, as though planning out his future curses. About line 21 he can begin to speak with power.

†T.J.B. Spencer has written on Shakespeare's Greece in '"Greeks" and "Merrygreeks"', *Essays on Shakespeare and Elizabethan Drama,* edited by Richard Hosley, 1963.

The Sun is blessedly creative; but since Timon's tragic reversal, opposites have come into force, and destruction is invoked. The good is beautifully defined before rejection. Timon proceeds to more denunciation. Timon's naked figure asserts the excellence of humankind before despising it:

> Who dares, who dares
> In purity of manhood stand upright,
> And say, 'This man's a flatterer'? If one be,
> So are they all. For every grize of fortune
> Is smooth'd by that below. The learnèd pate
> Ducks to the golden fool: all's obliquy.
> There's nothing level in our cursed natures
> But direct villainy. Therefore be abhorr'd
> All feasts, societies, and throngs of men!
> His semblable, yea, himself, Timon disdains.
> Destruction fang mankind.

(IV.iii.13)

At 'yea, himself' Timon's hands take in his own figure, previously, at 'purity of manhood', impressive. As to man's crooked (obliquy) nature, Timon is perfectly right; that *is* how men behave, the best as well as the worst of us; his eyes have simply been opened to the truth. His demand, as the word 'level' indicates, has always expected a simple perfection, not to be found on earth. He is now, and henceforth, at home only among the elements. He moves from Sun to Earth:

> Earth, yield me roots!
> Who seeks for better of thee, sauce his palate
> With thy most operant poison! What is here?
> Gold! Yellow, glittering, precious gold! No, gods,
> I am no idle votarist. Roots, you clear heavens!

(IV.iii.23)

At 'Ha, you gods, why this?' Timon laughs. What gold he finds is not clear. It is to take on symbolic properties, and is best not as caskets or coins, nor as gold-dust, but rather as solid nuggets, of different sizes. 'Who seeks for better of thee' appears to point to mining for mineral wealth, and that, in fact, is what Timon finds he has done.

It may be distantly looking ahead to Goethe's 'mine-folk' in Part II of
his *Faust,* to Wagner's *Ring of the Nibelungs,* and to Ibsen's *John
Gabriel Borkman.* It may be regarded as a natural product, as what
we may call 'earth-gold'. It is also regarded, here and elsewhere, as
specifically the gift of the gods. We may, borrowing a phrase from
The Winter's Tale (III.iii.127), call it 'fairy gold', or, perhaps better,
'tragic gold'. A possible source is in Lucian's *Timon Misanthropos.*
   He addresses it as a curse on man:

> This yellow slave
> Will knit and break religions, bless the accurs'd. . .
>
> (IV.iii.33)

It is the 'common whore of mankind' that 'putt'st odds among the rout
of nations' (IV.iii.42), but it also visually, and in its use in the action,
serves as a symbol of Timon's worth, drawing men still to him. Louis
MacNeice's poem 'Circe', on the in-built riches of Narcissistic
self-concentration, contains the words 'Timon kept on finding gold.'
   Alcibiades enters with his soldiers. Alcibiades we have met before
as a guest of Timon, and also in a scene with the Senators of Athens,
inserted within the early acts in order to help the later relation of
Timon's story to communal issues; for Alcibiades has been disgusted
with the Athenian government, and is now leading an army against his
countrymen. Timon addresses him:

> I know thee too, and more than that I know thee
> I not desire to know. Follow thy drum.
> With man's blood paint the ground, gules, gules.
> Religious canons, civil laws are cruel.
> Then what should war be?
>
> (IV.iii.57)

Scorn of war's childish ritual beats in Timon's

> I prithee, beat thy drum and get thee gone.
>
> (IV.iii.96)

Hearing that Alcibiades is warring against Athens, he is ambivalently
approving, and gives him gold to pay his troops:

> *Timon.* Warr'st thou 'gainst Athens?
> *Alcibiades.*   Ay, Timon, and have cause.
> *Timon.* The gods confound them all in thy conquest; and
> Thee after, when thou hast conquer'd!
> *Alcibiades.*   Why me, Timon?
> *Timon.* That, by killing of villains thou wast born to conquer
> My country.
> Put up thy gold: go on – here's gold – go on.
> Be as a planetary plague, when Jove
> Will o'er some high-vic'd city hang his poison
> In the sick air. Let not thy sword skip one.
> Pity not honour'd age for his white beard,
> He is a usurer. Strike me the counterfeit matron;
> It is her habit only that is honest,
> Herself's a bawd. Let not the virgin's cheek
> Make soft thy trenchant sword, for those milk-paps
> That through the window-bars bore at men's eyes,
> Are not within the leaf of pity writ,
> But set them down horrible traitors. Spare not the babe
> Whose dimpled smiles from fools exhaust their mercy. . .
>
>   (IV.iii.102)

Timon's lines have a two-way effect on us, since each reference is loaded with the pity and horror it surmounts. The sanctities of religion, beautifully defined, do not escape:

> Put armour on thine ears and on thine eyes,
> Whose proof nor yells of mothers, maids, nor babes,
> Nor sight of priests in holy vestments bleeding,
> Shall pierce a jot. There's gold to pay thy soldiers.
> Make large confusion, and thy fury spent,
> Confounded be thyself! Speak not, be gone.
>
>   (IV.iii.124)

He abjures alike the conquered and the conqueror. The condemnation is wholesale.

Alcibiades is accompanied by two ladies whom Timon regards as whores, and gives gold to, while loading his speeches with sexual disgust. To this extent, we can say that the Shakespearian pattern of the Sonnets, where the will to a homosexual idealism is accompanied by

heterosexual lust, is followed in *Timon of Athens;* and we remember
Lear's speeches of sexual horror, which, like Timon's, seem to
obtrude a little unsuitably from the objective story. Timon, as a man
is best regarded as supersexual, as sexually uninvolved, though virile;
he is compared to the bisexual 'Phoenix' (II.i.32). These passages
may be regarded as 'personal' Shakespearian comments. *Timon of
Athens* shifts between the personal and the universal without
overmuch regard to particularities of characterisation. Shakespeare
is generally ready to work beyond characterisation, if the
occasion demands it.

When alone, Timon addresses the Earth:

> That nature, being sick of man's unkindness,
> Should yet be hungry! Common mother, thou
> Whose womb unmeasurable, and infinite breast,
> Teems and feeds all; whose self-same mettle,
> Whereof thy proud child, arrogant man, is puff'd,
> Engenders the black toad and adder blue,
> The gilded newt and eyeless venom'd worm,
> With all the abhorrèd births below crisp heaven
> Whereon Hyperion's quickening fire doth shine,
> Yield him, who all thy human sons doth hate,
> From forth thy plenteous bosom, one poor root!
>
> (IV.iii.177)

Shakespeare knew the disgust felt at nature's 'abhorrèd births', as is
witnessed by Leontes' lines on the spider in *The Winter's Tale*
(II.i.38-44); and often enough elsewhere. Small creatures especially
seem to arouse this in us, and sometimes make us feel that nature is
evil; in which we are presumably wrong. In *The Ancient Mariner*
Coleridge's hero is saved by his sudden awareness of the water-snakes'
joyous beauty. Shakespeare shows both approaches. In *Measure for
Measure* we hear:

> And the poor beetle that we tread upon
> In corporal sufferance finds a pang as great
> As when a giant dies.
>
> (III.i.77)

And in *Pericles:*

> The blind mole casts
> Copp'd hills towards heaven, to tell the earth is throng'd
> By man's oppression; and the poor worm doth die for't.

> (I.i.100)

We are, in such passages, reminded of William Blake. Now Timon's soliloquy accepts these 'abhorrèd births' as cared for equally with 'arrogant man' by the 'common mother', Earth. Nowhere else in Shakespeare is this apprehension given so extended a development. Timon's nature mysticism digs deep.

He continues by praying that the Earth shall bring forth only 'new monsters' of ferocity to replace 'ingrateful man' (IV.iii.189-91).

Apemantus, who has functioned hitherto as a misanthropic critic of Timon's generosity and human trust, comes to visit Timon, and has a long dialogue with him. Shakespeare seems to be at pains to justify his hero without quite knowing how to. Apemantus makes many good points. More, he is given a speech of noble nature-poetry:

> What! think'st
> That the bleak air, thy boisterous chamberlain,
> Will put thy shirt on warm? Will these moss'd trees,
> That have outliv'd the eagle, page thy heels,
> And skip when thou point'st out? Will the cold brook,
> Candied with ice, caudle thy morning taste
> To cure the o'er-night's surfeit? Call the creatures
> Whose naked natures live in all the spite
> Of wreakful heaven, whose bare unhousèd trunks
> To the conflicting elements expos'd,
> Answer mere nature, bid them flatter thee...

> (IV.iii.222)

All nature is reviewed in these latter scenes: trees, animals, earth, sun, sea. Our attention is here drawn to the sufferings of animals under a cruel heaven.

Apemantus regards Timon as a fool, who has merely adopted his new way of life enforcedly, not in principle. Timon answers that he had been a great prince and had fallen from his place through man's iniquity, whereas Apemantus is a nonentity who has no cause to hate men. The argument will scarcely appeal to us, and Wyndham Lewis in *The Lion and the Fox* was not far out when he

regards it as stating simply 'I am a tragic hero and you are not', which
is hardly an argument. The dialogue is not wholly satisfactory. We
have to regard Timon as noble and reluctant to hate, and Apemantus
as one who enjoys seeing what is bad. Perhaps the most interesting part
of it is Timon's speech on animals:

> *Timon.* Wouldst thou have thyself fall in the confusion of men,
>   and remain a beast with the beasts?
> *Apemantus.* Ay, Timon.
> *Timon.* A beastly ambition, which the gods grant thee to attain
> to. If thou wert the lion, the fox would beguile thee; if thou wert
> the lamb, the fox would eat thee; if thou wert the fox, the lion
> would suspect thee, when peradventure thou wert accused by the
> ass; if thou wert the ass, thy dulness would torment thee, and
> still thou livedst but as a breakfast to the wolf; if thou wert the wolf,
> thy greediness would afflict thee, and oft thou shouldst hazard thy
> life for thy dinner; wert thou the unicorn, pride and wrath would
> confound thee and make thine own self the conquest of thy fury;
> wert thou a bear thou wouldst be killed by the horse; wert thou a
> horse, thou wouldst be seized by the leopard; wert thou a leopard,
> thou wert german to the lion, and the spots of thy kindred were
> jurors on thy life. All thy safety were remotion, and thy defence
> absence. What beast couldst thou be, that were not subject to a
> beast? and what a beast art thou already, that seeest not thy loss
> in transformation!

> (IV.iii.325)

Why Shakespeare treats his animals here in so heraldic and distanced
a style, I do not know. Perhaps, if treated at first hand, they would
have proved too vital for this depressing account. The thought is
at times strange, relying on traditional folklore, but the general
tenor is clear. The animal creation is regarded as suffering. Not only
do animals live in a semi-consciousness ('dullness'), but they are
at the mercy of their own hunger (the wolf's 'greediness'; cp.
'belly-pinchèd wolf', *King Lear,* III.i.13), and of destruction, every
instant of their existence a hazard; which is true enough when we
regard nature, as Tennyson puts it, 'red in tooth and claw' (*In
Memoriam, LVI*). Our faith in a beneficent universe is clouded.
Timon rejects not only man, but the animal creation whose plight

is worse.*

Timon is left alone:

> I am sick of this false world, and will love nought
> But even the mere necessities upon't.
> Then, Timon, presently prepare thy grave.
> Lie where the light foam of the sea may beat
> Thy grave-stone daily. Make thine epitaph
> That death in me at others' lives may laugh.

(IV.iii.378)

This is our first mention of the sea. The Sea functions among our other elements as a primary symbol, and needs to be effective in production, its surf sounding at appropriate moments throughout. Timon's speech continues with an address to his new-found gold:

> O thou sweet king-killer, and dear divorce
> 'Twixt natural son and sire! thou bright defiler
> Of Hymen's purest bed! thou valiant Mars!
> Thou ever young, fresh, lov'd and delicate wooer,
> Whose blush doth thaw the consecrated snow
> That lies on Dian's lap! Thou visible god,
> That solder'st close impossibilities,
> And mak'st them kiss! that speak'st with every tongue
> To every purpose! O thou touch of hearts,
> Think, thy slave man rebels, and by thy virtue
> Set them into confounding odds, that beasts
> May have the world in empire!

(IV.iii.384)

The gold makes a two-way statement. Here perhaps Timon caresses, fondles, it before the final repudiation. It is conceived as a great power, and is given poetry, not all ironic, concerning its power; it is also satirical; but, in action, it acts as a visible symbol, together with Timon's nakedness, of a compelling excellence. It makes Timon still sought after, it is one with his magic.

---

*For other thoughts on the 'beast' references in *Timon of Athens,* see Willard Farnham, *Shakespeare's Tragic Frontier* (Oxford 1973; originally USA 1950), II.

His next visitors are the Poet and Painter. This scene I take here, heralded by Apemantus' 'Yonder comes a poet and painter' (IV.iii.358), which must mean that it was meant – at one stage of the composition anyway – to follow, though in the Folio it is placed later. The Poet and Painter were earlier conceived as sensible exponents of their arts, but now appear as heavily satirised flatterers. This is not necessarily a dramatic weakness. As the drama's perspective shifts, lesser people may be differently presented: we are asked to accept people according to what the particular scene demands. This is unusual in Shakespeare, though something similar happens with Wolsey in *Henry VIII*. The dialogue is on a fairly obvious plane. They flatter Timon for his gold; he is for once cautious and guards it suspiciously. The incident is Shakespeare's way of saying that all artists are likely to be trivial as persons. Byron thought this, and called the pen 'that mighty instrument of little men' (in *English Bards and Scotch Reviewers*, II.4).

More important is Timon's meeting with Flavius, his former steward, who comes to help him. He is forced to admit one good man among the race he has denounced:

> Had I a steward
> So true, so just, and now so comfortable?
> It almost turns my dangerous nature mild.
> Let me behold thy face. Surely, this man
> Was born of woman.
> Forgive my general and exceptless rashness
> You perpetual-sober gods! I do proclaim
> One honest man, mistake me not, but one;
> No more, I pray, and he's a steward.

(IV.iii.499)

Notice how Timon talks to the gods as though he were on the same level; this is part of the conception of him as superman. The words remind us of Abraham talking to Jehovah of Sodom and Gomorrah. He gives Flavius gold from his god-given stores:

> Look thee, 'tis so. Thou singly honest man,
> Here, take. The gods, out of my misery,
> Have sent thee treasure. Go, live rich and happy.
> But thus conditioned – thou shalt build from men,

> Hate all, curse all, show charity to none,
> But let the famish'd flesh slide from the bone
> Ere thou relieve the beggar; give to dogs
> What thou deny'st to men. . .

(IV.iii.532)

Timon here enjoys the possession of mysterious, god-sent, gold. He handles, almost caresses it, with pride. Gold is good or bad according to its use. Out of Timon's suffering Flavius is to be made happy; we recall Romeo and the Apothecary, and his man Balthasar. The gold acts on many levels, here illustrating the advantage to another person of the tragic experience of the protagonist. The last words, spoken as Timon's hand is drawn down his bare body, convey a horror of human suffering together with a Nietzschean surmounting of that horror. (For Nietzsche see *Thus Spake Zarathustra,* IV.20; see also my *Christ and Nietzsche,* pp.171-2). This is a general characteristic of Timon's curses.

I place next the visit of the Bandits. Strictly, it should have come, according to the Folio text, before that of Flavius; but we have already, with at least some evidence, moved the scene with the Poet and Painter, and that may leave us a free hand with this. There are advantages in placing it here. It makes a good climax. The scenes as they follow each other are in danger of being static, and to be true to Shakespeare's usual method we do well to make our climax here, before the final movement.

The Bandits are drawn to Timon by his gold. They say that they are 'men that much do want', and Timon replies:

> Your greatest want is, you want much of meat.
> Why should you want? Behold, the earth hath roots;
> Within this mile break forth a hundred springs;
> The oaks bear mast, the briers scarlet hips;
> The bounteous housewife, nature, on each bush
> Lays her full mess before you. Want! why want?

(IV.iii.422)

We need to interpret the general tenor of such speeches, and this is clearly a vegetarian counsel. The speech was used by Roy Walker in his work on vegetarianism, *The Golden Feast* (1952). Timon — and Apemantus too — have already shown sympathy with animals and their sufferings (page 127 above). I quote a passage from *The Essene Gospel of John,* translated by E.B. Szekely and quoted by M.H. Tester in *Two Worlds* (October 1973):

> Jesus answered: 'Thou shalt not kill, for life is given to all by God, and that which God has given, let no man take away, for I tell you truly, from one mother proceeds all that lies upon the earth; therefore he who kills, kills his brother and from him will the earth mother turn away, and the flesh of slain beasts in his body will become his own tomb. Kill neither man nor beast nor yet the food that goes into your mouth, for if you eat living food the same will quicken you; but if you kill your food, the dead food will kill you also, for life comes only from life, and from death comes always death. . . So eat always from the table of God, the fruits of the trees, the grains and grasses of the fields, the milk of the beasts, and the honey of the bees. For everything beyond these is Satan, and leads by the way of sins and disease unto death.'

I do not write myself as a propagandist for a complete vegetarianism on these grounds, since there are so many minute life-forms that have to be killed; but I suspect there may be a truth here. Byron thought meat dangerous: 'Meat I never touch, nor much vegetable diet. . .I should not so much mind a little accession of flesh — my bones can well bear it. But the worst is, the devil always came with it. . .' (Journal, 17 November 1813; *Letters and Journals,* II, pp.327-8). However, Jesus, according to the Gospels, accepted fishing.

What we can say, is that Timon in his nakedness is being thrown back on elemental simplicity at every turn, and here states it firmly; assuming, as others have, that meat is not a natural human need at all. He proceeds to praise the Bandits for being what they profess:

> Yet thanks I must you con
> That you are thieves profess'd, that you work not
> In holier shapes; for there is boundless theft
> In limited professions. Rascal thieves,
> Here's gold. Go, suck the subtle blood o' the grape,
> Till the high fever seethe your blood to froth,
> And so 'scape hanging. Trust not the physician —

His antidotes are poison, and he slays
More than you rob. Take wealth and lives together.
Do villainy, do, since you protest to do't
Like workmen.

(IV.iii.431)

The attack on physicians looks ahead to Bernard Shaw. Many in our
own time distrust an over-reliance on drugs, preferring nature-cures
of one kind or another.

There follows a remarkable poetic extravagance, urging, it would
seem, that private property is not rooted in the universal scheme
which only exists by give-and-take, as indeed Timon tried to exist
in his days of prosperity. Or again, the cosmic bodies may be
seriously being charged with thieving. The passage is ambiguous.
What is however most important, is the chance given for enlisting
and describing the cosmic powers:

> I'll example you with thievery.
The sun's a thief and with his great attraction
Robs the vast sea; the moon's an arrant thief
And her pale fire she snatches from the sun;
The sea's a thief, whose liquid surge resolves
The moon into salt tears; the earth's a thief
That feeds and breeds by a composture stolen
From general excrement.

(IV.iii.441)

In production, I have favoured a diurnal change in the lighting,
starting with dawn, proceeding to midday, with sunset for Flavius,
and now moonlight. Night suits the surreptitious entry of the
Bandits, and Timon can make great effect in this speech, his naked
body catching the moon's light from above, and using gestures freely.
Before the reference to the sea, there is naturally the sound of
surf, to which Timon listens for a moment; the speech need not be
taken too quickly. Meanwhile the Bandits, who had looked for gold
only, are rather flabbergasted by this outpouring of great poetry,
and glance at each other in comic vacancy. Timon's cosmic speech
can itself be spoken lightly, with more than a touch of humour.
Comedy is quite in place, but there is profundity too. Timon
urges them to steal. The laws themselves have 'uncheck'd theft':

Rob one another. There's more gold. Cut throats.
All that you meet are thieves. To Athens, go –
Break open shops. Nothing can you steal
But thieves do lose it. Steal no less for this
I give you – and gold confound you howsoe'er!

(IV.iii.451)

Again, the words can be spoken lightly, ironically, even with humour,
until the end. 'Confound': he rejects them, while urging them on. It
was the same with Alcibiades and war. He is a partly ironic counsellor
of violence, whilst remaining untouched by it himself, and antagonised
by it. Exactly how far irony is behind his counsel one cannot say; for
him, it may not be there; for Shakespeare, and we who read, it is.
Anyway, the result is, paradoxically, that he reforms the thieves:

> *Third Thief.* He has almost charmed me from my profession, by
>   persuading me to it.
> *First Thief.* 'Tis in the malice of mankind that he thus advises us,
>   not to have us thrive in our mystery.
> *Second Thief.* I'll believe him as an enemy, and give over my trade.
> *First Thief.* Let us first see peace in Athens. There is no time so
>   miserable but a man may be true.

(IV.iii.457)

This is our one explicit example of Shakespeare's handling of the
morality of tragedy. *Timon of Athens,* you see, is tragedy becoming
fully conscious, both of itself and its effect. Here we see how Timon's
nihilism does not, in fact, have a nihilistic result. Alcibiades earlier
decided to take Timon's gold, but not his 'counsel' (IV.iii.130-1).
Timon's magical personality acts on Alcibiades and the Bandits; his
poetry acts on us. There is, in the very nature of tragic poetry, its
own *katharsis,* or purification.

We must not in reading forget Timon's nakedness. Great care must
be taken for its artistic projection. In the wild scenes he wears,
presumably, a rough loin-cloth. The stripping of the body is an
extension of the more purely imaginative stripping of surfaces
throughout the greater tragedies to show the inward organs of
existence, as I have described in *The Wheel of Fire,* 'Tolstoy's
Attack on Shakespeare' (enlarged edition, pp.286-7). Leading up to
Timon we have Edgar's appearance in *King Lear:*

Lear. What! Have his daughters brought him to this pass?
Could'st thou save nothing? Did'st thou give them all?
  Fool. Nay, he reserved a blanket, else we had been all shamed.

(III.iv.62)

Contemporary practice expected some sort of costume, though Lear's
following reference to a 'forked animal' suggests a more scanty
covering than 'blanket':

Lear. Why, thou wert better in thy grave than to answer with
thy uncovered body this extremity of the skies. Is man no more
than this? Consider him well. Thou owe'st the worm no silk, the
beast no hide, the sheep no wool, the cat no perfume. Ha! Here's
three on's are sophisticated; thou art the thing itself.
Unaccommodated man is no more but such a poor, bare, forked
animal as thou art. Off, off, you lendings! Come, unbutton here.
  Fool. Prithee, nuncle, be contented. 'Tis a naughty night to
swim in.

(III.iv.103)

It is interesting to find death ('grave') already, before *Timon*,
associated with nakedness. The approach is simultaneously
denigratory and positive: naked man is both the poorer and yet
more essentially real, or true, for his state.

It is the same with Timon. Nudity is ambivalent. It may be
regarded as reductive, as when we are told that Timon 'will be left a
naked gull' after flashing as a 'phoenix' (II.i.31-2). Apemantus refers
to Timon's 'slave-like' and 'sour-cold' habit (IV.iii.206,240). Flavius
asks, 'Is yond despis'd and ruinous man my lord?' (IV.iii.468). And
yet Timon's appearance should be simultaneously impressive. At
'who dares in purity of manhood stand upright' followed by 'His
semblable, yea himself, Timon disdains' (IV.iii.13,22) there is surely
reference to a fine visual impact. The truth is, nudity always and
inevitably has a two-ways pointing; like the god-given gold which
Timon digs up, at once cursed as the cause of evils and yet serving to
build up Timon's stature and even suggesting, symbolically, the gold
essence of his personality. His nakedness acts in much the same way,
indicative of the human essence; like Milton's Adam in 'naked majesty'
(*Paradise Lost,* IV.290). Timon represents a state before the Fall, or
some super-state beyond it; what Timon, thinking of a painting, calls
'almost the natural man' (I.i.158), a phrase which B.L. Joseph relates to

'the innocence of unfallen man', while also urging us – though he does not himself favour Timon – to visualise the original performer in action (*Elizabethan Acting*, 1951, pp.111-12). Other parts of Milton's description are relevant, especially perhaps this:

> His fair large front and eye sublime declar'd
> Absolute rule; and Hyacinthin locks
> Round from his parted forelock manly hung
> Clustering, but not beneath his shoulders broad.

> (IV.300)

This may be allowed to suggest Timon's appearance; especially, if we put 'leonine' for 'Hyacinthin', for his hair. More relevant still is Milton's nation, at the close of *Areopagitica*, 'raising herself like a strong man after sleep and shaking her invincible locks'. This, and Samson too, matches Shakespeare's conception (the passages are discussed in my *Poets of Action*).

The naked Timon with his new-found gold and wholsale condemnation of mankind generates, in his setting, a personality of magical status. The visual impact complements, and sometimes directly counters, his words with a statement far beyond them: the words alone are certainly not enough. His body confronts man with the human essence, which has been wronged by human iniquity. The actor in his nakedness, and through him Timon, radiates power. He should infuse power into every instant of his physical stance (see our frontispiece). This alone prevents the later scenes from appearing undramatic. Little gesture is required. The body should speak: this is the quintessence of acting. It is as a supreme exhibitionism, but it is more than that; it is prophetic.

Shakespeare, thinking in terms of Jacobean stage practice, may have been baffled by the problems raised. He may have thought the play unactable, and this may have been why he left it unrevised for staging (H.J. Oliver, Arden edition, p.xviii). I have discussed the practice of stage nudity in our own time in 'The Body Histrionic', *Shakespearian Production* (enlarged).

In *Christ and Nietzsche* (p.227-8) I wrote (references are to *Thus Spake Zarathustra*):

Zarathustra, in talking variously of the 'spirit of poetry' lusting 'to show himself naked' (IV.14) – remember Shelley's peculiar and recurring emphasis — and of the Superman rejoicing 'to bathe his nakedness' in a 'burning sun of wisdom' where gods are 'ashamed of all clothing' (II.21), has defined a tension and resultant corresponding closely to Timon's story. Just as Hamlet aims to settle his problems by play-production, Timon becomes an actor, his return to naked savagery driving to the limit one aspect of the exhibitionist urge, which is really the impulse towards self-universalisation, dormant within all histrionic and poetic power. The integrated superman is, as in the New Testament, driven back on such a simple giving of himself; and, just as the crucified Christ challenges through the centuries man's self-seeking head-culture not by argument nor even alone by poetic speech, but pre-eminently by his body, so Timon, through a dramatic conception of staggering simplicity recalling the contrast of coin and human life in *The Merchant of Venice,* hurls at man not only metallic gold but also the other golden powers of the human form.

Religious associations naturally cluster (for the Crucifixion, see pages 146, 165 below). We may remember that King David incurred criticism for indecent exposure while dancing before the Ark to the glory of God: 'And I will make myself even more lightly esteemed than this, and I will become low in my eyes' (2 Samuel, VI.14-22; and see 1 Chronicles, XV.29). 'Low': there is an ambivalence about it, as though God's glory were man's shame; as indeed it may often be.

Timon's denunciations are Hebraic. A sermon by the Reverend Kenneth Leech in *The Times* (27 April 1974) drew attention to the part played by nakedness in the story of Isaiah, who in order to enforce his message lived so for three years (Isaiah, XX, 2-4; compare Micah, I, 8); and also of St Basil the Blessed in Russia. William Blake in *The Marriage of Heaven and Hell,* 'A Memorable Fancy', wrote: 'I also asked Isaiah what made him go naked and barefoot three years? He answered: "The same that made our friend Diogenes, the Grecian."' Diogenes may be naturally compared with Timon.* Mr Leech draws a fine distinction between conventional appearance, which is of the Devil as Lord of Lies, and the revelation of the true contours of life, which may be, or seem, a madness, but is simultaneously prophetic.

---

*For a discussion of Montaigne's comparison between the legendary Timon and Diogenes, see Willard Farnham, *Shakespeare's Tragic Frontier,* pp.65-7 (quoting Montaigne); also pp.72-4. See H.J. Oliver, Arden edition of *Timon of Athens,* XL note.

The body, says Christ, is more than clothes (Luke, XII.23).
William Blake understood that. Truth is seen best when 'naked' (V.i.72)

He is like Prometheus, or Oedipus. Oedipus fits well, as in
Sophocles' second play he is sought after by Thebes, which had
formerly rejected him; for his magic would be powerful in death,
could they have his body buried there; but he will not return. So too,
Athens sends a delegation of Senators to Timon in the wilds,
imploring his return, to accept absolute power and to save the
city from Alcibiades. Athens had been ungrateful:

> Forgetting thy great deeds, when neighbour states
> But for thy sword and fortune, trod upon them. . .
>
> (IV.iii.94)

Timon's virtues were generally recognised, as by the Stranger (page 117).
Flavius had shown 'duty and zeal to your unmatched mind'
(IV.iii.525). Timon, we know, had superb qualities; but now they
attain a higher status of almost supernatural power. The public
body, which is seldom known to 'play the recanter' (V.i.151), abases
itself before the individual. If he returns to Athens, Athens may yet
be saved.

What follows is best as a night-scene. Timon appears first
silhouetted, as a dark figure, on the rocks. The Senators confess the
City's crime and implore his forgiveness, and aid. This we must see
as the key scene in *Timon of Athens*. Timon is a beyond-communal
figure, before whom the community is abased. If this does not suit
what we suppose to be the impact of earlier scenes, we must adjust
our reception of those scenes to make sense of this climax. What the
Senators say of Timon *must* be true; his presence *can* help them;
they, being in the play as we are not, are in a position to know
more of the matter than we are. Shakespeare has done what he can
throughout to assure an adequate response on our part: the rest is
our responsibility.

Timon turns to the Senators, catching henceforth enough light
for the purpose. He is adamant:

> Well, sir, I will. Therefore I will, sir, thus —
> If Alcibiades kill my countrymen,
> Let Alcibiades know this of Timon,
> That Timon cares not. But if he sack fair Athens,

> And take our goodly aged men by the beards,
> Giving our holy virgins to the stain
> Of contumelious, beastly, mad-brain'd war,
> Then let him know, and tell him Timon speaks it,
> In pity of our aged and our youth,
> I cannot choose but tell him that I care not,
> And let him take't at worst; for their knives care not
> While you have throats to answer. For myself,
> There's not a whittle in the unruly camp
> But I do prize it at my love before
> The reverend'st throat in Athens. So I leave you
> To the protection of the prosperous gods
> As thieves to keepers.

(V.i.173)

Observe, again, the pity that beats within the phraseology: 'goodly' and 'holy', as against 'mad-brain'd war'. Every sweetest and noblest value is maintained, before being surmounted. These are the virtues that mankind has desecrated, and cannot therefore plead in its cause. Timon speaks as a being from another world, condemning: he is like Nietzsche's Superman who to men would appear 'terrible in his goodness' (*Thus Spake Zarathustra,* II.21). Tennyson's lines in *Maud* (2.I.ii) might have been Timon's:

> Arise, my God, and strike, for we hold Thee just,
> Strike dead the whole weak race of venomous worms
> That sting each other here in the dust;
> We are not worthy to live.

Flavius says, 'Stay not. All's in vain', and Timon proceeds:

> Why, I was writing of my epitaph.
> It will be seen to-morrow. My long sickness
> Of health and living now begins to mend,
> And nothing brings me all things.

(V.i.190)

We remember Richard's emphasis on 'being nothing' (page 34 above). Life's meaning has changed, and death is embraced. 'Nothing' must be read as the 'Nirvana' of Oriental mysticism. A few words on 'Nirvana' may be here in place.

In his dying Timon attains selfhood, that 'To be' for which Hamlet craved. I quote from S. Radakrishnan's *Indian Philosophy* (1923; edition of 1929). 'It was not', he writes, 'the intention of the Upanishads to make of the deeper self an abstract nothingness. It is the fullest reality, the completest consciousness and not a mere negative calm'. The logic of thought has in it a 'negative movement, where it rises by the repudiation of the finite, but this is only a stage in the onward march. By the negative process the self has to recognise that its essence is not in its finitude or self-sufficiency. By the positive method it finds its true self in the life and being of all. All things exist within this true self.' (Part I, iv, p.162). In death 'it is the false individuality that disappears while the true being remains'. Our life 'builds an individuality and isolates itself from the stream of being. In deep sleep these barriers are broken. Nirvana is getting back into the stream of being and resuming the uninterrupted flow'. Only since it is beyond the horizon of human thought we are obliged to employ negative terms to describe it. To think that Nirvana is annihilation is according to Buddha a 'wicked heresy' (Part II, vii, pp.449-50

This is the philosophy on which Nietzsche built *The Birth of Tragedy*. The Dionysian music takes us to the 'I' which is 'from the abyss of being', and is not man as we apprehend him, 'but the only verily existent and eternal self resting at the basis of things' (5). In tragedy we enjoy watching the world of phenomena conducted to its boundaries 'where it denies itself, and seeks to flee back again into the bosom of the true and only reality' (22). 'Being' is our key concept.

Middleton Murry, writing of Macbeth's great speech (*Discoveries*, as before; page 100 above), says that in the 'anger and contempt' of his 'rejection of life' there is 'exaltation also'; we are 'uplifted'; and he assumes that Shakespeare — for as we have seen, he takes the lines as expressing Shakespeare's own thought — has a 'positive' vision behind them: 'He rejects this life because he knows of something better and truer. . . He has a memory of some kind of experience beside which the actual experience of life is indeed trivial.' This 'experience' he relates to *The Phoenix and the Turtle;* and I have related *Timon of Athens* to the Sonnets. In John Cowper Powys's *Rodmoor* (the first English edition recently published by Macdonald and Co.) a 'Nirvana' experience is directly related by the book's hero to what I call the 'seraphic' vision in Baptiste. 'Spinoza', he says, 'worshipped only one thing, that which is beyond the limit, beyond the extremest verge, beyond the point where every living thing ceases to exist and *becomes nothing*.' It is 'a blinding white light which puts out all the candles and all the shadows of the world':

> 'I call it white light', he continued, 'but really it's not light at all, any more than it's darkness. It's something you can't name, something unutterable, but it's large and cool and deep and empty. . . It stops all the sickening tiredness of having to hate things. It'll stop all my longing for Baptiste, for Baptiste is *there*. Baptiste is the angel of that large, cool, quiet place. Let me once destroy everything in the way and I get to Baptiste — and nothing can ever separate us again!' (*Rodmoor*, 1973, p.326).

Like Timon he dies by the sea, as an approach to his Nirvana.

Timon is on the brink of a great, undefinable mystery that *'mends'* his life with 'all things'. We must allow as much, or more, right to 'all' as to 'nothing'.* Except at a moment when he has temporarily lost his poise, 'You only speak from your distracted soul' (III.iv.116), there is — with the exception of one of his two epitaphs† — no talk of Timon's soul, since he is conceived as one who has attained to true 'being', from which the soul-self is not distinct.

It is right that *Timon of Athens,* which is a summation and rationalisation of all Shakespeare's sombre tragedies, should alone give us a philosophic reading of death. In Shakespearian tragedy death has never existed as a simple negation. It is the same in Ibsen: 'In death', he wrote in *Brand* (V), 'I see not overthrow.' Death is as a needed completion, to cover the wholeness of human existence, corresponding with Christ's words on the cross, *'Consummatum est'*. Perhaps Christianity has been part of it, since we do not have quite the same

---

*We might compare Henri Bergson's contention that 'the idea of absolute Nothing' is, 'at bottom, the idea of Everything' (*Creative Evolution*, translated by Arthur Mitchell, 1928, p.312). For Shakespeare's use of 'nothing', a vital Shakespearian word, see my *The Crown of Life,* 82 note; also *The Sovereign Flower*, General Index B, VI Miscellaneous 'Nothing'.

†For the problems raised by the epitaphs, which were provisionally copied from Shakespeare's source (Plutarch), see the Arden edition, edited by H.J. Oliver, pp.139-40, note; also the New Penguin edition, edited by G.R. Hibbard, Commentary, p.253.

effect in Greek tragedy. The Shakespearian treatment is profound and
rational. Men must die some time, and tragedy offers us an action
which leads up to death, and illustrates different ways of dying.
Without it, we should be left with a partial study only, and feel
cheated and depressed, as we are perhaps in *Troilus and Cressida.*
In romantic comedy there is certainly a place for the 'happy ending',
but it has in it always an element of make-believe, at least unless we
see it as reflecting a truth of happiness beyond, or within, death.
Perhaps Shakespeare saw it like this, and in his latest work devised
plots that seemed to say as much.

And so Timon is now, after a fashion, less uncompromising. He
recognises, like Macbeth, the agonising paradox of mortal existence:

> Commend me to them.
> And tell them that, to ease them of their griefs,
> Their fears of hostile strokes, their aches, losses,
> Their pangs of love, with other incident throes
> That nature's fragile vessel doth sustain
> In life's uncertain voyage, I will some kindness do them.
> I'll teach them to prevent wild Alcibiades' wrath.

(V.i.202)

The intended expedient, as Timon next demonstrates, is suicide. This
is, in part, seriously meant. It is a statement of the human plight, firm
as far as it goes, in close attunement to the Duke's long speech on
death in *Measure for Measure* (III.i.5-41), and is directly in line
with Timon's own 'nothing brings me all things'. Timon's thoughts
are now only on death:

> Come not to me again, but say to Athens,
> Timon hath made his everlasting mansion
> Upon the beachèd verge of the salt flood,
> Who once a day with his embossèd froth
> The turbulent surge shall cover. Thither come,
> And let my grave-stone be your oracle.
> Lips, let sour words go by, and language end;
> What is amiss, plague and infection mend.
> Graves only be men's works and death their gain!
> Sun, hide thy beams! Timon hath done his reign.

(V.i.219)

I see him here as having loosened his loin-cloth, and now as flinging it
down to mark his severance from humanity. If he is completely naked,
the lights should dim on him below the waist, since complete frontal
nakedness for a male is dramatically weak, there being no control over
the sexual organ, which flaps about regardless. Better to wear a small
gold covering, suggesting Timon's soul-worth taken into death; which
has been my own expedient in the recital.

Timon, who in his Feast scene was entertained by a masque
celebrating the Five Senses, would now, at this last hour, have the
world of sense-perception blacked out, though the sea, probably
through its sound, serves as some sense-equivalent to his 'Nirvana'.
His grave is to act as an 'oracle': that is, as a reminder of the desecration
of love and generosity. He is here almost forgiving. 'Sour words' are
passed. That there may be good in human life is allowed by 'what is
amiss'; that only is to incur destruction. So much said, 'graves' are
best and in death is 'gain' whatever it may be. In my full productions
I had difficulty with the 'sun'. Using a night-scene, I felt it was
inapposite, and rashly changed it to 'stars', which I do not in retrospect
think right. 'Sun, hide thy beams' does, in fact, exactly suit my
reasons for wanting a night-scene here, and can be spoken naturally
enough. Timon turns away, his hands raised to his eyes, blotting out
the world of manifestation; and the back view, shown full length,
appears completely naked; then, as the light dims, it becomes a
silhouette only; and so we leave him as a lone and majestic figure
against the night sky. Or we may end with a fade-out and the sound
of surf: for the end in my recital, see pages 163-6 below.

The action is framed by Alcibiades' final entry, receiving the
keys of the surrendered city. A soldier brings him a copy of Timon's
epitaph from where he is

Entomb'd upon the very hem o' the sea:

Here lie I, Timon, who alive all living men did hate.

Pass by, and curse thy fill, but pass, and stay not here thy gait.

(V.iv.66-73)

How Timon died, and who buried him, is not stated, nor is it necessary
that it should be. As with Sophocles' Oedipus in the *Oedipus Coloneus,*
the super-hero is gone, we do not know how. Alcibiades does full
justice to his memory, regarding him as one inhumanly, or superhumanly,
beyond human griefs:

These well express in thee thy latter spirits.
Though thou abhorr'dst in us our human griefs,
Scorn'dst our brain's flow and those our droplets which
From niggard nature fall, yet rich conceit
Taught thee to make vast Neptune weep for aye
On thy low grave, on faults forgivon. Dead
Is noble Timon, of whose memory
Hereafter more. Bring me into your city,
And I will use the olive with my sword,
Make war breed peace, make peace stint war, make each
Prescribe to other as each other's leech.
Let our drums strike.

(V.iv.74)

No other tragic hero in Shakespeare has so nobly conceived and
meaningful a conclusion. Especially notice its universal quality, the
personal story enlarged by the ending to general issues. But indeed
those general issues have been in Timon throughout the last acts.
His survey of human inadequacy has been mainly an impersonal
survey. Based on man's presence on earth and his simple needs, it
denounces one after another of his civilised vices, ranging widely. It
sets man in his place in the cosmos, among the elements and the
trees and beasts of nature, and bound for death. It is Shakespeare's
attempt to make a comprehensive survey of the human plight, and
he does it by imagining, in descent from earlier protagonists, a
semi-superhuman figure. Timon is man's futurity, what man must
measure himself by in order to advance. His manifold rejections
may be felt as provisional. I find an apposite passage, quoted by
Glen Cavaliero in *John Cowper Powys: Novelist* (1973, p.186),
from an unpublished portion of Powys's *Porius,* where Taliessin
is described as:

A Being set apart from others to reveal to the world what only
poetry *could* reveal, that is to say, a certain secret life of
planetary sensation, totally independent of love and religion and
nationality and power and fame and glory and learning, a life of
sensation that lifted the elements to the level of vegetation,
vegetation to the level of animals, animals to the level of men,
and men not only to the level of one another but to the level of
the immortal gods. (*Porius,* 186)

That is not unlike the consciousness in which Timon lives in the final acts. True, he sees the created scheme as a 'false world' (IV.iii.378), and living as a 'sickness' (V.i.191); but it is because he cannot limit his generous consciousness to the scheme of finite creation that he craves for his Nirvana. Meanwhile, this massive survey of nature and human existence may be the clearer from the viewpoint of rejection.

It has been my purpose to show how and in what precise way *Timon of Athens* is pre-eminent among the tragedies. Its faults are obvious, and seem to be due to Shakespeare having put it aside, unrevised, as Una Ellis-Fermor thought.* The staging can remedy this easily enough. The early scenes are carefully constructed, and gripping; the more important later scenes need much help with atmospheric appeal. Timon's ñakedness, being in itself powerful, needs less reliance on gesture than is usual, except at certain points. The actor's whole body should act, at every instant, radiating power; and his stances should be well-spaced, and firm. He is challenging society as much with his body as with his words. He should be given fine, leonine, hair. Much should also be made of his gold, given, as Timon says (IV.iii.26-30; 533), by the gods. Timon should on occasion show pride at possessing it. If the play be done like this, we shall not talk so much of 'faults'.† I have written of *Timon of Athens* in book after book, perhaps most cogently in *Christ and Nietzsche* (pp.223-9), but never so fully as here. I quote from Thomas McFarland's *Shakespeare's Pastoral Comedy* (University of North Carolina Press, 1972, p.127):

> It is not unfitting that *Timon of Athens* should seem so important a play in the estimation of G. Wilson Knight. For, although one cannot wholly agree with his high estimate of it as a work of art, there can be little doubt that its emotional attitudes represent, in extreme form, the most powerful and pervasive of Shakespeare's dramaturgic conceptions.

Hazlitt said much the same, that it was of all Shakespeare's plays the one where he was most 'in earnest'. Muriel Bradbrook has in

---

*See Una Ellis-Fermor, *'Timon of Athens*; An Unfinished Play', *Review of English Studies,* XVIII, 1942, now available in her *Shakespeare the Dramatist,* edited by Kenneth Muir, 1961. For an excellent recent discussion of how *Timon of Athens* may have been composed, see the New Penguin Shakespeare edition of the play, edited by G.R. Hibbard ('An Account of the Text', pp.255-62).
†I have offered a point-by-point description of my own productions in an extended essay in *Shakespearian Production* (enlarged, 1964).

Shakespeare the Craftsman (1969) written an extended appreciation. It is not quite true that I regard it as a perfected work of art, though I may have given that impression. It reminds us rather of Tolstoy's repudiation of art in his later parables, or of Powys and Lawrence when they say that their novels are less art than propaganda. Writers do sometimes think like this, and in such a mood *Timon of Athens* may have been composed. Shakespeare, to put it bluntly, wanted for once to speak out and unburden his soul.

The ranging importance and wide survey of the drama can be seen from the number of plays that have since been composed on the subject, many of them relying on Shakespeare's influence; its influence on future dramatists has been far greater than that of any other Shakespearian play. The two halves of *Timon of Athens*, representing false society and romantic severances are variously used, either in separation, or both together. These I have recorded in '*Timon of Athens* and its Dramatic Descendants' in *Shakespeare and Religion*, 1967, pp.211-21; see also *The Golden Labyrinth* (throughout). These dramatists are working over anew the material of *Timon of Athens*. Romantic drama is elsewhere deeply concerned with Shakespeare's works, analysing the implications self-consciously, as with Oswald in Wordsworth's *The Borderers*, who reads like an Iago who understands his own motives, and their meanings. Byron's plays, too, are studied and self-consciously manipulated workings out of Shakespearian themes, *Sardanapalus* especially (see my *Poets of Action*, pp.222, 237-8). Allardyce Nicoll wrote wisely when he, thinking perhaps of *Manfred* and *Sardanapalus,* called *Timon of Athens* 'Byronic' (*Shakespeare,* 1952, p.61).

Even more important is the correspondence of Byron as a man to Timon. He called his early *Childe Harold* a 'sketch of a modern Timon' (1813 Preface to *Childe Harold*), and his life, in the context of the Europe of his day, is strikingly illustrative. Byron, set between radical revolutionaries and an effete aristocracy, is closely analogous to Timon's rejection of Apemantus on the one side and the Senators on the other. Both put wealth to the cause of military action. Since Byron is so historically significant a figure, we can say that *Timon of Athens* forecasts, not only the future of British drama, but the social and political history of Great Britain. The 'usury' (III.v.101) of the Senate, together with Timon's invectives against avarice, are clear forecasts of capitalism. In Byron we have the same original benevolence as in Timon, the same rejection by his community, the same part-militant and part-pacific attitude to revolution, the same financial crash followed by recovery of wealth, the same satiric attacks on time-serving poets, the same retreat after exile to the sea and expectance of burial beside it; and much else. Looked at deeply, if we see through externals into the true lines of force, Byron lives out the story of Shakespeare's Timon. All this I have described in my book, *Byron and Shakespeare*.

Timon's superman status points us to Byron's *Manfred* and Shelley's *Prometheus Unbound;* as also to Matthew Arnold's *Empedocles on Etna*. Herman Melville drew power from the terms 'Timonism' and 'Timonised' in *Pierre* (see Lewis Mumford, *Herman Melville*, IX). I am told that Dostoievsky was attracted by it; and Professor Kenneth Muir, in his *Shakespeare's Tragic Sequence*, 1972 ('Timon of Athens', p.189), draws attention to Karl Marx's discussion of Timon's speeches on gold. (See also Kenneth Muir's '*Timon of Athens* and the Cash Nexus', *Modern Quarterly Misc.*, 1947, pp.57-76). It is also Nietzschean. Timon's rejection, in bodily strength, of humanity, contrasts with the Crucifixion of Christianity. The view implied is that of Nietzsche's critique of man: 'In gazing on tragedies, bullfights, and crucifixions hath he hitherto found his best happiness on earth' (*Thus Spake Zarathustra*, III.13). Timon's end might be supposed to constitute a similar critique (see page 165 below). Perhaps this is why Shakespeare, fearing its boldness, left the play unrevised.

Timon of Athens should be readily understood by the troubled youth movements of our day in their dissatisfaction with the world as we know it, and its Buddhist-like conclusion. Probably the prophetic nature of the play has something to do with its faults, if they be faults. Shakespeare may have put it aside prematurely, thinking it a failure, though the truth is that he was writing before his time, and almost out of his depth. *Timon of Athens* relates as well to Sophocles' *Oedipus Coloneus* as to Byron; to the Greek Prometheus as to Shelley's; it overspans, and outspans, the centuries.

7 THE LAST PHASE

It will be obvious that Shakespeare's development after the sombre tragedies can be easily placed. The tragedies had laid a firm basis in spiritual experience, and that experience was next exploited in various ways.

The two Roman dramas, *Antony and Cleopatra* and *Coriolanus,* return to a more or less normal treatment of heroism, though in *Antony and Cleopatra* that heroism is presented through a glorified sense of love-irradiation, which so illuminates the action that the world appears semi-transcendental, at least in the poetry. Antony has his expectance of meeting Cleopatra in Elysium (IV.xii.51), and Cleopatra's end is given its visionary splendours; in her dream of Antony (V.ii.79-92), recalling Romeo's dream (page 41 above), and in her dying. In this, her story has an early analogy in that of Cassius in *Julius Caesar,* who moves from a doubtfully approved plotter to a fine death, his story at its close being graced by love (page 62 above). *Coriolanus* shows a tragic rise of importance, from Coriolanus' iron-plated soldiership and pride to the sudden collapse of those values in his surrender, in love and duty, to a mother's plea, with a sudden reversal of overpowering force.

The plays that follow, of which Clifford Leech regarded *Timon of Athens* as a 'harbinger' (*Shakespeare's Tragedies,* etc., London, 1950, VI), are impregnated by a kind of mysticism that we need not here discuss. All I am concerned in this book to say is that, in so far as we find such properties in them, they develop directly from Shakespeare's tragic sequence, which had, as I have been at pains to show, its own spirituality, in so far as we attend to the poetry. In my essay 'Gloucester's Leap' (page 111 above) I suggest that Gloucester's fall and miraculous survival in *King Lear* enacts what may be the truth of death, along the lines I have designated in *Atlantic Crossing* (p.27). The last group can be considered as an even more elaborate concentration on poetry, or myth: in them Shakespearian poetry tends to direct the plot. They are exploitations of what he had won in his comedies and tragedies, blending them to make strange works on the brink of mysticism. This group of final plays is heralded by *Pericles,* again a Greek story (Shakespeare seems to have turned to the Greeks when searching for new adventures), and is followed by *The Winter's Tale, Cymbeline, The Tempest,* and *Henry VIII* (studied in my *The Crown of Life*). In *Pericles* and *The Winter's Tale* what Nietzsche would call the 'Dionysian' plunge into the womb of Being, or Nirvana, is given a more Apollonian emphasis in Pericles' reunion with his wife and daughter, and the statue-scene of Hermione's resurrection. Sculpture, in Nietzsche's scheme, is an Apollonian art. In *The Tempest* Prospero is an assured superman developing earlier tragic heroes' poetic magic and Timon's personal radiations into a real magic, imaginatively, even fancifully, apprehended. Timon's sense of human baseness is repeated in Prospero's; for both are severed from their community. The nature emphasis in *Timon of Athens* is developed into the nature-magic of Prospero and Prospero, too, has his Nirvana, or something very like it, in his 'cloud-capp'd towers' speech (IV.i.148-58), compared by Middleton Murry, in the essay I have referred to, with Macbeth's 'Tomorrow and tomorrow and tomorrow. . .'. When Prospero says:

> Though with their high wrongs I am struck to the quick,
> Yet with my nobler reason 'gainst my fury
> Do I take part: the rarer action is
> In virtue than in vengeance. . .

> (V.i.25)

he might be thinking back to, and reversing, the line taken by Timon; though one might be forgiven for suggesting that one would rather be the recipient of Timon's salutary curses than of Prospero's forgiveness.

At the end Shakespeare returns in *Henry VIII* to a national theme, with, in the scene where the Angels come to welcome Queen Katharine to Paradise, a Christian sense of immortality, in contrast to *Timon of Athens* and *The Tempest. Henry VIII* may be regarded as an act of humility and self-surpassing, in which Shakespeare writes beyond his personal instincts; though for many of us today Timon's, and Prospero's, Nirvana way of thought may be the more congenial. Or we may prefer Caliban's wonderful lines (III.ii.147-55) on a spiritualised island, or universe.

PART 2: THE PERFORMANCES

My lecture-recitals 'Shakespeare's Dramatic Challenge' have been of
two kinds. In England, Canada and the United States, during the
years 1972 to 1975, they were given in ordinary clothes, interspersing
lecture commentary with dramatic readings and dramatic action. As
they developed, more and more emphasis fell on the acting, and when
I was invited by Mr Geoffrey Reeves to give performances at the
Northcott Theatre in Exeter, I decided, as before with *This Sceptred
Isle,* on a greater amplification. Hitherto *Timon of Athens* had not
had the emphasis which was needed. Though it was the culmination
to which all else moved, it came last, when there was too often little
time, and this for a play which few knew and which accordingly
needed more in the way of explanation. So, when the Northcott
invitation came, I decided to expand the recital from about 1¼ hours
to 1¾ hours or even, with an interval, 2 hours. The added time was to
be given to an expanded account and performance of *Timon of Athens.*
This version was first tried out at Queen Elizabeth School, Crediton,
on the invitation of Dr Raymond Skinner and Mr Vivian Summers,
followed directly by the three performances at the Northcott Theatre.

These presentations involved, for *Timon,* effects of costume, or
lack of costume, atmospheric lighting, and sound effects. All this was
not new to me: I had done the whole play in Toronto in 1940 and at
Leeds in 1948, and the last scenes, which I now chose, were like those
that had featured in my 1941 recital at the Westminster Theatre,
London, *This Sceptred Isle* (described, as were my full-length
productions, in my *Shakespearian Production*). Now, having so
decided, I also made the rest of the recital conform to the extent of
using slight costume changes: an auburn wig for Richard III, Richard II,
Romeo, and Hamlet, with corduroy jacket and trousers and an open
shirt; and then, for Othello, Macbeth and King Lear, first a
fawn-coloured gown, lent me by Mr Vivian Summers, and later a
green overcoat (made in Finland), which I had in regular use; also a
Star of David (given me by Dr Miriam Halevy, of Israel). For two
of these I wore a red sash, and a fur cap, with no wig, though for
Lear I discarded the cap and used a cord instead of the sash.

For Timon, I used at first my own hair, though later I improved the

151

performance by wearing an impressive wig, which served to make him less of an anguished prophet and more like a middle-aged angel of judgement. Before he threw off his clothes, I used at different times various costumes, including a robe lent me by Mrs Freda Jenkins and for the video noted below one devised by Mrs Mary Valentine , ending up with a gold dressing gown I possessed, which was easy to pack and looked suitably rich, especially when supplemented by my C.B.E. medallion.

I used a stick freely, for various purposes: for Richard III's lameness, Richard II's attack on his antagonists, for the Apothecary in *Romeo and Juliet* and for the early part of *King Lear;* also for Timon's chasing of his false friends and later as a spade for his digging. No elaborate properties were needed, nor scenic effects except a higher level, or platform, and, when available, a few objects placed as a non-realistic background. At the Northcott Theatre I was greatly helped by Miss Mary Evans, who acted as my stage-manager and general assistant.

A video-tape has been made, and is now being remade, at Yeovil, presented by Mr Derek Valentine and directed by Mr Simon Mauger of Yeovil College, to whom requests for information regarding hire or purchase should be sent.* First I used my own hair for Timon; the wig came into my performance later, starting with that at the Gulbenkian Centre, Hull University, at the invitation of Professor Raymond Brett and Mr Donald Roy, in March 1976. At Hull I was presented with rolls of gold paper, which I used there, and subsequently, to make Timon's gold. A video-tape was made at Hull.

Three performances were given on the invitation of Dr Ann Jennalie Cook for the International Shakespeare Association Congress at Washington, in April 1976. Another was done on the invitation of Mr James Redmond, for Westfield College, University of London, and the Central School of Speech and Drama, in July. There are to be repeat performances at the Northcott Theatre during the coming autumn.

I should also note a performance for the Open University organised by Olivia Mordue, now Mrs Anderson, at Stockwell College of Education, Bromley, through the kindly collaboration of

---

*I have also recently been given a video-tape made from my shorter version (omitting — by a misfortune — *Timon of Athens*), as delivered at the University of Northern Colorado at Greeley, Colorado, in 1975.

Dr Audrey Insch, in March 1976; together with the shortened
version for the Ripley Poetry Association, Bromley. These were
generously reviewed by Mr Norman Harvey in *The Kentish (Bromley)
Times*; I might add that the first was attended by Michael
Bampton, the Apemantus of my 1948 Leeds *Timon of Athens*.

To supplement this factual record, I append Olivia Anderson's
impressionistic account. She had accompanied me and Mr Fred
Cannan on my American tour in 1975 and so was pretty well
saturated in the recital before the Northcott performance,
which is the subject of her present review, written for the *Exeter
University Club Bulletin,* where it appeared in January 1976.

Wilson Knight at the Northcott

On the eve of the publication of his biography of his brother,
Wilson Knight at the age of 78 gave three ninety-minute
performances of astonishing power, humour and interest at the
Northcott Theatre, Exeter, in November 1975.

'If Jackson Knight is Vergil, then Wilson Knight is Shakespeare',
someone once said, and watching him on stage he was, in truth,
the living embodiment. His message was simple: 'Shakespeare's
tragic heroes rise and do *not* fall, at the end, whatever their
circumstances'; in acting 'Attend to the poetry and the rest will
emerge in its own right'.

The title of this recital was 'Shakespeare's Dramatic Challenge'.
At its close one felt that the actor-scholar had taken up the
gauntlet and that after a life-time devoted to producing, acting in
and writing about the plays, the challenge for him had been
answered.

For the purposes of the recital Wilson Knight relied on few props,
though lighting and sound were important. In corduroy jacket and
trousers with an auburn wig to mask his identity he talked first
of Richard III who went out to do battle in the name of good and
evil, St George *and* the dragon; the amused response from the
audience increased when he said that it mattered not, in this
context, whether Richard was going to Heaven or Hell, provided
that dramatically and poetically, he made a good end, which he did:

'Let us to't pell-mell. If not to heaven, then hand in hand
    to hell'.

For Richard II the speaker flung a piece of red velvet across his shoulder for the royal poetry. He contrasted Marlowe's Edward II (a similarly weak king, grovelling in a filthy dungeon and coming to a 'sticky', miserable, bad end) with the dignity of Richard II whose tone and gesture will make his accusers shrink back, at asking him to sign so base a confession. He defends himself but is at last slain. 'Mount, mount my soul! Thy seat is up on high, whilst my gross flesh sinks downward here to die.' A fine exit.

For Romeo the velvet was removed. An academic gown was thrown across the shoulder to suggest the increase in stature when Romeo had matured as a man. A walking stick was Romeo's rapier, later used by Lear, and then a spade by Timon, digging for roots in the wilderness. For Othello, Macbeth and Lear, Wilson Knight donned a long fawn robe, red sash and fur hat he had bought for a recent Canadian tour.

After the interval he appeared in colourful robes with his C.B.E. for Timon's trappings of power. Drums of Alcibiades' army heightened the drama. Later the atmosphere was intensified by swishing surf. The ragged, leather loin-cloth, worn first by Wilson Knight thirty-five years ago, was admirable for Timon in the wilds, and when this was shed, the briefer, gilt covering was perfect as Timon dissolved in fading light.

'Poetic' is the adjective which best describes his style of acting: 'Attend to the poetry. . .'. 'Do not ask what kind of man Macbeth is, and then proceed to act him accordingly'. This is not to deny the importance of character study and other factors; these will emerge through the poetry. The jerky, nervous lines spoken by Macbeth before Duncan's murder are not easy to deliver:

'If it were done when 't is done, then 't were well

It were done quickly'

— a humorous pause, almost a groan from Wilson Knight as he labours, showing us the actor's difficulty.

Romeo, likewise, tries the actor's skill. At the beginning of the play his poetry is weak, moreover he has the unenviable task of speaking upstage in the balcony scenes, but as Romeo grows as a man, the poetry grows in beauty — 'It was the lark, the herald of the morn. . .', and in this speech Wilson Knight maintains that despite Romeo's sorrow his face should light up, his voice be lighter in saying the words 'jocund day'; they demand it. His face puckered as he tried to say them with a whimpering sob, the ridiculous effect bringing laughter from the audience. Romeo is by now a man; he kills Tybalt as much by the fury of his poetry with one blow, and fifteen are not necessary, or however many some actors choose. 'This shall determine that.'

In *Romeo* Wilson Knight gave us a vivid cameo as the old Apothecary (much liked by a schoolgirl I talked to in the interval). The lady on my left found his Lear superb in tone and gesture, with just enough thunder. Shakespeare's mixture of great poetry and the colloquial was beautifully illustrated in Lear, I thought, with 'Come on, my boy. How dost, my boy? Art cold? I am cold myself.'

An American student from Connecticut found the whole performance a memorable experience. Others will no doubt have their favourite illustrations. My own preferences change from time to time as I look back on the performance, with the exception of *Timon*, the key play to which a third of the programme was devoted. The gruff tones, the angle of the shoulder, at once wild and graceful, remain with me. Timon is of our age with hippies and inflation and it is surprising that, although Wilson Knight's *The Wheel of Fire* with its general interpretation of the character appeared in 1932, it is only now that more people are appreciating the play.

Critics might say that Wilson Knight belongs to the old school of poetic traditional actors, now out of fashion. Yet such comment can be set aside as one recognises important principles in what he suggests. His genius makes his argument sound simple, a matter of commonsense. His instruction for acting is clear, though its execution is difficult. No actor alone, or pure academic, could have revealed so much of Shakespeare's art. The audience responded to his knowledge and skill. The fact that he was 60 years older than Romeo was not uppermost in the mind. They were listening to Shakespeare's poetry as never before. The only concession he made to his age was at one point when he did not fall to the ground, saying his advisers were against it but that he used to fall beautifully in the past!

So towards the end of his life, after 30 books of literary interpretation, one play about the Incas (precursor of Shaffer's

Royal Hunt of the Sun), numerous articles and lecture offprints,
Wilson Knight, the old stager, returns to his first love – Shakespeare's
Dramatic Challenge.

Olivia Mordue,
Senior Counsellor, London Region of the Open University

I next present the text of my selections from *Timon of Athens*. The
whole performance was in two parts, with an interval between, *Timon
of Athens* constituting Part II. My choice of passages has the merit of
variety, and lends itself to changes in the acting. For a valuable
adjustment in my use of commentary, I am indebted to a suggestion
made to me by Mr Geoffrey Reeves. My ending was newly devised:
the discarding of Timon's loin-cloth had not been part of my earlier
Timon performances. Its importance is indicated at the conclusion
of my text.

PART II OF SHAKESPEARE'S DRAMATIC CHALLENGE

Italics are used for (i) Commentary, read or spoken, and (ii) Lines
incorporated from another scene. My additions to the text are in
square brackets. Stage directions are in capitals.

WEARING TIMON'S RICH CLOTHES, INCLUDING A
GOLDEN GOWN, WITH A MEDALLION AND A
BROWN-GOLD WIG.

*We now give excerpts from the final scenes of 'Timon of Athens'.
This play sums up and explains Shakespeare's sombre tragedies. It
is a generalised and universal tragedy, showing a princely aristocrat –
the name 'Timon' suggests 'honour' or 'worth' – of generous heart,
who is a public benefactor, entertains lavishly and helps all in distress.
We are shown a grand feast. Then, his wealth exhausted, he solicits
help from his friends, who turn him down, one after the other. His
eyes are opened to human ingratitude and greed. He invites them to
another feast. They think that he has recovered his wealth and
expect a glorious party. There is a long table, like that in the
picture of Christ at the Last Supper. Timon speaks a grace of
withering sarcasm, overturns the table, seizes a staff and belabours
his guests, like Christ with the money-changers in the Temple.
Then he casts from him the trappings of civilisation, vows universal*

hatred of man, and retreats in part-nakedness to the wilds. He has been
jerked up to a state beyond mankind.

The setting is then changed to a line of rocks, beyond which we
hear the surf of the sea. Timon is first a silhouette, by night, and
then gilded by the dawn. Digging for roots to eat, he finds gold.

From now on, he confronts those who visit him with curses against
man's vices; but also with (i) the gold, which we may call, with a
phrase used elsewhere in Shakespeare, 'fairy gold', and which suggests
Timon's infinite stores of spiritual wealth: and (ii) with his naked
body, suggesting the essential humanity which man has desecrated;
like the Old Testament prophet, Isaiah, who went for three years
naked to enforce his message.

Shakespeare is ranging beyond his period. It is our vices, today,
that are being attacked. Like many of our own young people, Timon
contracts out of society through dissatisfaction with its greed and
lusts, its false morality and international crimes. Like them, he would
live close to nature; and also like them, he turns to Oriental thought,
longing for his 'Nirvana' in death, the perfect state of Buddhism,
wherein 'nothing' is said to bring him 'all things'. He wishes to be
buried by the sea. No cause of his dying is given us; we simply
watch him dissolve into the ocean of being.

IN WHAT FOLLOWS OTHER PERSONS AND THE TABLE
ARE LEFT TO THE IMAGINATION. TIMON USES A
STICK TO DRIVE OFF HIS FRIENDS AND LATER AS A
SPADE. GOLD IS PRESENT BUT WHAT HE GIVES MAY
BE IMAGINED; OR TIMON CAN THROW IT OFF-STAGE.
(STAGE RIGHT, LEFT AND CENTRE ARE INDICATED
BY CAPITALS: STAGE RIGHT IS AUDIENCE'S LEFT).

Commentary, addressed to audience: *We now go back to the second
feast, where Timon breaks up the party.*

FEAST SCENE. FULL LIGHTS.

You great benefactors. For these my present friends, as they are
to me nothing, so in nothing bless them, and to nothing are they
welcome.

Commentary: *He overturns the table or tables, seizes a staff and
belabours his friends.*

LIGHTS LOWER. CRASH OF CROCKERY. BEATS GUESTS.

You knot of mouth-friends! Live loath'd and long,
Most smiling, smooth, detested parasites!
What, dost thou go? Soft. Take thy physic first. Thou too —
    and thou.
What, all in motion? Henceforth be no feast
Whereat a villain's not a welcome guest.

FINGERS HIS MEDALLION; THEN, DISGUSTED, REMOVES
IT. TEARS OFF CLOTHES PIECE BY PIECE. ALL BUT
TRUNKS.

Nothing I'll bear from thee
But nakedness, thou detestable town.
Take thou that too, with multiplying bans!
Timon will to the woods, where he shall find
The unkindest beast more kinder than mankind.
Burn house! Sink Athens! Henceforth hated be
Of Timon, man and all humanity.

STAGE CLEARED. LOW MUSIC OR SURF.

BARE STAGE WITH PLATFORM C. SOME OBJECTS AS
BACKGROUND. GOLD, COVERED, DOWN L.

NIGHT. SURF. TIMON ON PLATFORM C. SILHOUETTE.
THEN HIS BODY, FROM R, IS GILDED GRADUALLY BY
THE RISING SUN. HE WEARS A ROUGH LEATHER
LOIN-CLOTH, ONE SIDE SHORT, WITH A TASSELLED GOLD
CORD; A SMALL SUN-SYMBOL ON A GOLD NECKLACE; AND
HIS BROWN-GOLD WIG TO CATCH LIGHTS.

O blessed breeding sun, draw from the earth
Rotten humidity; below thy sister's orb
Infect the air!

FULL LIGHT.

            Who dares, who dares,
In purity of manhood, stand upright (STANDING FIRMLY)
And say 'This man's a flatterer'? If one be
So are they all. The learned pate

Ducks to the golden fool. All's obliquy.
There's nothing level in our cursed natures
But direct villainy. Therefore, be abhorr'd
All feasts, societies, and throngs of men!
His semblable, yea himself, Timon disdains (GESTURES TOWARDS
Destruction fang mankind!   HIMSELF).

    TIMON DIGS, DOWN L.

        Earth, yield me roots.
Who seeks for better of thee, sauce his palate
With thy most operant poison. What is here?

    NUGGETS OF GOLD ARE DISCOVERED. TIMON LAUGHS.

Gold! Yellow, glittering, precious gold! No, gods,
I am no idle votarist. Roots, you clear heavens!
Ha! You gods, why this? (AGAIN LAUGHING) What this, you
   gods, why this
Will lug your priests and servants from your sides,
This yellow slave
Will knit and break religions, bless the accurs'd.
Come damnèd earth,
Thou common whore of mankind, that putt'st odds
Among the rout of nations. . .

    FONDLES GOLD ALMOST LOVINGLY. AFTERWARDS
    BITTER.

        O thou visible God, thou touch of hearts,
Think thy slave man rebels, and by thy virtue
Set them into confounding [strife], that beasts
May have the world in empire.

    DRUM DISTANT.

        Ha! a drum.
I'll bury thee. Nay, stay thou out for earnest.

    DRUM NEARING, R. GROWS LOUDER, STOPS. FROM
    NOW ON VARIOUS PEOPLE ARE IMAGINED TO
    ENTER FROM R.

Commentary (addressed to audience): *Alcibiades and his Army come in.*

[What am I?]
I am Misanthropos and hate mankind.
I know thee too, and more than that I know thee
I not desire to know. Follow thy drum.
With man's blood paint the ground, gules, gules.
Religious canons, civil laws, are cruel;
Then what should war be?
I prithee, beat thy drum (SCORNFULLY) and get thee gone.

Commentary: *Alcibiades offers Timon money.*

[Money?] Keep it. I cannot eat it. Warr'st thou against Athens?
The gods confound them all in thy conquest,
And thee after, when thou hast conquer'd.
Put up thy gold: go on — here's gold — go on.
Be as a planetary plague, when Jove
Will o'er some high vic'd city hang his poison
In the sick air. Let not thy sword skip one.
Pity not honour'd age for his white beard;
Put armour on thine ears and on thine eyes,
Whose proof nor yells of mothers, maids, nor babes,
Nor sight of priests in holy vestments bleeding
Shall pierce a jot. There's gold to pay thy soldiers (HURLING
Make large confusion, and thy fury spent   GOLD) —
Confounded be thyself! Speak not. Be gone.

DRUMS. THEY GROW DISTANT, AND FADE. LIGHT
SOFTENS. LOW SURF. TIMON SETS OUT THE GOLD IN
DISPLAY, THEN DISMISSES IT.

I am sick of this false world and will love nought
But even the mere necessities upon it.
          Common mother, thou,
Whose womb unmeasurable and infinite breast
Teems, and feeds all,
Yield him, who all thy human sons doth hate,
From forth thy plenteous bosom, one poor root!

DIGS, L. SURF HAS ENDED. SUNSET SUGGESTION.

O, a root! Dear thanks. (LIES DOWN) More man. Plague, plague.
Away! What art thou?

Commentary: *Flavius has come to help and serve him, sharing what
wealth he has.*

Had I a steward
So true, so just, and now so comfortable?
It almost turns my dangerous nature mild.
Let me behold thy face. Surely, this man
Was born of woman.
Forgive my general and exceptless rashness
You perpetual-sober gods! I do proclaim
One honest man — mistake me not — but one.
How fain would I have hated all mankind.
And thou redeem'st thyself. But all, save thee,
I fell with curses.

    TIMON REFUSES MONEY.

Look thee: thou singly honest man,
Here, take. The gods, out of my misery,
Have sent thee treasure.

    TIMON HANDLES HIS GOLD PROUDLY AND GIVES SOME
    TO FLAVIUS.

               Go, live rich and happy.
But thus condition'd — thou shalt build from men,
Hate all, curse all, show charity to none,
But let the famish'd flesh slide from the bone (HAND ON RIBS)
Ere thou relieve the beggar. Be men like blasted woods
And may diseases lick up their false bloods:
And so farewell and thrive. Stay not.

    HIS FEARFUL WORDS ARE IN PART COUNTERED BY
    HIS GOLD, HIS GLINTING HAIR AND GENERAL APPEARANCE
    (see page 135 above). SURF LOW.

Then Timon, presently prepare thy grave.

MOVES ON TO PLATFORM C. SURF STRONG BUT SHORT.

Lie where the light foam of the sea may beat
Thy grave-stone daily: make thine epitaph
That death in me at others' lives may laugh.
More things like men!

MOONLIGHT.

Commentary: *Bandits enter. They have heard Timon has gold. They approach saying 'We are not thieves, but men that much do want.'*

TIMON AT FIRST GUARDS HIS GOLD SUSPICIOUSLY.

Why should you want? Behold, the earth hath roots;
Within this mile break forth a hundred springs;
The oaks bear mast, the briars scarlet hips;
The bounteous housewife, nature, on each bush
Lays her full mess before you. Want! Why want?
Ye've heard that I have gold. Yet thanks I must you con
That you are thieves profess'd, that you work not
In holier shapes; for there is boundless theft
In limited professions. Rascal thieves,
Here's gold. Take wealth and lives together.

Commentary: *The thieves are baffled by his generosity and still more by the cosmic poetry that comes next, following Timon's actions and gestures with gaping faces.*

Do villainy, do, since you profess to do't,
Like workmen: I'll example you with thievery.

ON PLATFORM C. SPEAKS WITH A TOUCH OF HUMOUR.

The Sun's a thief and with his great attraction
Robs the Vast Sea; the Moon's an arrant thief,
And her pale fire she snatches from the Sun;
The Sea's a thief, whose liquid surge resolves
The Moon into salt tears; the Earth's a thief
That feeds and breeds by a composture stolen
From general excrement. Each thing's a thief.
The laws, your curb and whip, in their rough power
Have uncheck'd theft.

SPEAKING WITH LIGHT IRONY AND TOSSING GOLD
TO THEM.

Rob one another. There's more gold. Cut throats. All that you
meet are thieves. Break open shops; nothing can you steal but
thieves do lose it. Steal no less for this I give you; and gold
confound you howso'er!

LIGHTS UP FOR COMMENTARY. (NO GOWN WORN.)

*The result is curious. Timon's poetry has reformed the thieves. One
says, 'Has almost charm'd me from my profession, by persuading
me to it'; and another plans to give over 'his trade'. 'Charmed'; there
is magic in Timon's personality, and his words act on men not for
evil, but for good. He is now bound for death; but he is interrupted.
A deputation comes from Athens, imploring him to return; as in
Sophocles' 'Oedipus at Colonus', the hero who had been rejected
is wooed to return and bring his magic to save his City; but with
both – they are similar conceptions – it is too late.*

TIMON ADDRESSES SENATORS R.

Well, Sir; I will, therefore I will, Sir, thus –
If Alcibiades kill my countrymen,
Let Alcibiades know this of Timon,
That Timon cares not. But if he sack fair Athens,
And take our goodly aged men by the beards,
Giving our holy virgins to the stain
Of contumelious, beastly, mad-brain'd war,
Then let him know, and tell him Timon speaks it,
In pity of our aged and our youth,
I cannot choose but tell him, that I care not,
And let him take't at worst. So I leave you
To the protection of the prosperous gods
As thieves to keepers.

TIMON LOOSENS HIS LOIN-CLOTH AND HOLDS IT
DANGLING IN HIS LEFT HAND. LIGHTS LOWER
SLIGHTLY OR ARE CONCENTRATED WITH SHADOWS.
TIMON WEARS A GOLD SEX-COVERING. (HIS
ACTUAL GOLD IS NOW NO LONGER EVIDENT,

BEING INCORPORATED IN HIMSELF.)
TIMON GOES L UP STAGE A LITTLE, ASCENDING
PLATFORM C AND TRANSFERRING LOIN-CLOTH TO
RIGHT HAND. SPEAKS HAPPILY.

My long sickness
Of health and living now begins to mend,
And nothing brings me all things.

FLINGS LOIN-CLOTH DOWN, R, SEVERING HIMSELF
FROM MANKIND.

Come not to me again, but say to Athens,
Timon hath made his everlasting mansion
Upon the beachèd verge of the salt flood,
Who once a day with his embossèd froth
The turbulent surge shall cover. Thither come,
And let my grave-stone be your oracle.

TURNS L, AWAY FROM THEM.

Lips, let sour words go by, and language end;
What is amiss, plague and infection mend.
Graves only be men's works, and death their gain!

TURNS UP. BACK TO AUDIENCE. LIGHTS WITH SHADOWS.

Sun, hide thy beams! Timon hath done his reign.

TIMON RAISES HIS HANDS COVERING HIS EYES. AFTER
HIS WORDS, LIGHT DIMS TO SHOW HIM AS A
SILHOUETTE. SURF RISES. THEN COMPLETE FADE-OUT
WITH SURF BECOMING TUMULTUOUS. LIGHTS UP.
GOWN NOW WORN.

Commentary: *After 'Timon of Athens', Shakespeare moved on to
brighter plays: to 'Antony and Cleopatra', where reunion beyond death
is expected; to 'Pericles' and 'The Winter's Tale', where the dead
come mysteriously alive; to 'The Tempest', woven throughout of
magic; and to 'Henry VIII' with its vision of Paradise. Of this whole
movement, Timon is the turning point, the hinge or pivot.*

A note regarding the conclusion. The timing of the loosening and flinging down of the loin-cloth has varied, but is now fixed, as above. The brief covering is that depicted in my as yet unpublished *Symbol of Man*, but gilded, with glittering sequins. Sometimes I used the gold cord with it, draped across and left to fall on one side or both sides, with knots and gilded discs attached. Gold here (i) suggests Timon's super-sexuality, his status as a 'Phoenix' type (II.i.32), and (ii) relates back to his god-given 'tragic' gold, and denotes his soul-worth, taken with him to death. The action, from the discarding of the loin-cloth onwards, dramatises Timon's advance into what I have elsewhere called 'the immortal nakedness of death', 'the core of pure and naked significance' within 'the nothingness of death'; but with, at every stripping of his soul, 'an increase of his grandeur' (*The Wheel of Fire*, 1930, p.255; 1949, pp.232-3). 'Nothing' brings him 'all things'. That nakedness quite naturally holds spiritual or seraphic intimations may be felt from John Donne's lines in *Elegy XIX:*

> Full nakedness! All joys are due to thee.
> As souls unbodied, bodies uncloth'd must be,
> To taste whole joys.

As Timon turns away from us, he is in effect, since the narrow elastic at his waist scarcely registers, completely nude. Sounds and light are all-important. At Washington we had a tape (provided by Mr Joseph Zauner) of rising sea-tumult, within which sounded a horn, or siren, of vague but gripping suggestion.

The human image contrasts with the Crucifix of Christianity, which shows Christ twisted in agony, offering to us his tormented self, so both appealing to man's more dangerous instincts and aiming to reverse them. At Washington it was arranged that I should perform, with their kind permission, at Georgetown University in the Dahlgren (Jesuit) Chapel, where the walls around our open stage showed 14 relief figures representing the Stations of the Cross. The setting, if not in all respects dramatically suitable, was theologically appropriate, since it constituted a valuable comparison, besides receiving the blessings of tradition on my beyond-crucifixion, Nietzschean, advance. Timon, his locks glinting in the light and in full, undesecrated strength, is turned away from us. The back view has an esoteric reference, presenting, among other implications, the area of the Kundalini

Serpent of Buddhist teaching. As Timon's hands go up to cover his eyes at 'Sun, hide thy beams', the effect should resemble a Blake design. The Reverend Kenneth Leech, writing of the Crucifixion (*The Times,* 24 April 1976, p.14), quotes from St John of the Cross the phrase 'the dazzling darkness'. The phrase is even more appropriate for Timon's 'Nirvana'. In our dramatic action, as in this paradox, the whole nature of human tragedy is, in a flash, revealed. If lights and sounds are adequate, we have here the greatest stage moment conceivable. Dramatic art can go no further until some higher consciousness is developed. Till then, the human figure, under artistic treatment and shown on the brink of mystery, remains ultimate, the greatest image known to man; and it accordingly, being inexhaustible, spawns commentary; though written commentary, apart from the staged action and impact, does little, or nothing.

To return to our Christian analogy. We, as audience, are directly involved; and we have been rejected. Timon's naked body in perfect form contrasts not only with the Crucifix, but with all those broken and desecrated bodies of which the Crucifix is the summation, all the wars and sadistic horrors perpetrated by man throughout the centuries. Our iniquities are patent. No mediator, no saviour, is here offered. As Timon turns away, the responsibility is left with us. Yet more than sin is involved; 'health and living', the whole creation, seems at fault (pp.127, 138, 140-4 above; see also Romans, viii, 18-23). We are to probe deeper. Timon's dying is to be our 'oracle'. This, finally, is 'Shakespeare's dramatic challenge'.

APPENDIX: GRANVILLE-BARKER AND BEERBOHM TREE

A review of the collection *Prefaces to Shakespeare*, Vol. VI (edited by Edward Moore) in *The Times Literary Supplement*, 26 July 1974 (under a different title). Some minor adjustments are made.

In the story of Shakespearian production Harley Granville-Barker is a kind of Hamlet to the Claudius of Beerbohm Tree. He saw what was wrong, and did what he could to set it right. He succeeded in killing a great tradition, but failed to build on his success.

His fame rests on his three Savoy productions: *The Winter's Tale* and *Twelfth Night* in 1912 and *A Midsummer Night's Dream* in 1914. These created a sensation. Without proscenium arch or footlights, the action was thrown forward using a forestage, under straight and mainly uncoloured lighting. There was no painted scenery, only simple architectural effects and formal, solid objects and occasional use of coloured curtains. The aim was to throw the main emphasis on the text of the whole play with a swift run-on, and only what intervals were forced. The contrast with the sumptuous tradition built up by Charles Kean, Henry Irving and Beerbohm Tree was shattering, and the tradition was, in effect, shattered from then on.

Barker was influenced by William Poel, but unlike Poel, who favoured Elizabethan archaeology, his were modernistic displays with effects of *décor* and costume by Albert Rothenstein (Rutherston) and Norman Wilkinson that might well be called bizarre. They were far from colourless productions. His intention, wrote W. Bridges-Adams in *The Lost Leader* (1954), was to 'out-Poel Poel and out-Tree Tree in a single superb gesture'. Against the prevailing whiteness there was colour such as 'had never been seen in a theatre'. The music, based on folk music as arranged by Cecil Sharp, played an important part. The result was amazing. They remain among my most cherished theatrical memories: solid yet buoyant, bizarre yet graceful, and with a harmony that came near to magic.

Tree's defence of his productions is set out in 'The Living Shakespeare' and 'The Tempest in a Teacup' in his *Thoughts and After-Thoughts* (1913). They are distinguished pieces of writing, witty and in part convincing. What Tree was aiming at was a total theatre, using all the resources available. No one should attack Tree's methods without reading these defences. They have the light touch and delicate mastery of his best impersonations.

And yet Barker was, on the main issue, right. Picture scenery had to go; waits for scene-changes, cuts and rearrangements of the text were disastrous. The spectacular element in Tree's productions has since found a better medium in films. Barker's main contribution lay in salutary emphasis on an uncut text and rapid speech; also of great, perhaps chief, importance was the use of solid properties. Acting at the Savoy was strong: Ainley's Leontes was a leonine triumph, Lillah McCarthy's Viola spoke her 'willow-cabin' lines to fine effect and Dennis Neilson-Terry brought his family's charisma to Oberon. Soon after these successes, Barker left the stage and devoted himself to writing.

The present volume of uncollected prefaces (edited by Edward Moore) includes essays written as introductions to the three Savoy plays. They are adequate for the purpose but, lacking the original coloured illustrations, do little to match the magic that had been realised. In the second, Barker claims, against criticism, that he had been careful to vary the speed of the delivery. We have also two general essays of importance: one an 'Introduction to the Players' Shakespeare', first published in 1923 and 'From Henry V to Hamlet', a lecture to the British Academy, published in 1925, and two extended pieces, long out of print, from *The Players' Shakespeare,* on *Macbeth* (1923) and *A Midsummer Night's Dream* (1924).

These last contain astute comments on the details of the action. In the *Macbeth,* which Barker later said was 'full of blunders', he does well to emphasise Macbeth's courage before Banquo's ghost, but succumbs to the disintegrating scholarship rampant in his day by regarding the play's opening scene as spurious. Bridges-Adams, in a letter quoted by Robert Speaight in *William Poel and the Elizabethan Revival* (1954), wrote:

> Barker, I believe, had some brilliantly thought-out Witches at the blue-print stage when the war cut him short − but they might have proved to be the Witches of a man who didn't hold with Witches.

Barker's rejection of the opening is a disaster. One recalls Beerbohm Tree's 1911 production, with the Witches, or Weird Sisters, floating among smoky clouds and pitching their voices on a wailing note.

The poetry says that they 'hover through the fog and filthy air'; and they were shown doing it. This was a fine example of what I have elsewhere (*Shakespearian Production,* 1964, p.208) called Tree's 'spiritualized showmanship'. The first scene did not appeal to Barker: it did to Tree, whatever the scholars were saying; and here Tree was the more deeply Shakespearian of the two.

Barker's more famous *Prefaces* are as near to the academic world as to the stage. They abound in sharp insights and illuminating discussions of the text, but have little of the tang and flavour of the theatre. At their best, they add to our understanding of Shakespeare's problems and the way he met them; at the lowest, they seem to be playing only on the surface, while turning drama into narrative. After uncompromisingly asserting their academic importance, Barker's excellent biographer, C.B. Purdom, writes:

> That Barker got further from the stage and more deeply settled in his study as time passed the *Prefaces to Shakespeare* as a whole make evident. It was to be expected, for he had put himself on the wrong side of the curtain to complete the work he had set out to do.

The *Prefaces* were, however, necessarily in large part academic studies, and were presumably conceived as such.

Why did Barker retire from active stage work? There may be many reasons, but the one I offer is this: the greater plays had substances with which he was not at home. At the Savoy he had given us pastoral Shakespeare. The tragedies were waiting: he did, it is true, agree to a half-hearted collaboration with Lewis Casson and John Gielgud on *King Lear* in 1940, but was unwilling to give his name to it. According to Purdom, it had 'little of the real Barker quality' and was 'uncertain and confused'.

In an article contributed to *Drama* (New Series, 3; Winter 1946), Bernard Shaw says of Barker:

> His only other fault was to suppress his actors when they pulled out all their stops and declaimed as Shakespeare should be declaimed. They either underacted or were afraid to act at all, lest they should be accused of ranting or being *hams.*

According to Tree's biographer, Hesketh Pearson, 'Tree encouraged his actors to act, while Barker made his underact.' John Gielgud, however, writing of Barker's 1940 part-production in *Stage Directions* (1963), tells a different story: 'He encouraged grand entrances and exits centre-stage, a declamatory style, imposing gestures', all of which he ordered with 'unerring taste', avoiding the 'melodramatic'. Perhaps it all hinges on 'taste', on where we draw the line. Shakespearian tragedy demands in places *extravagant* acting: of this Barker says nothing, and we may assume that his practice was restrained.

He was for some reason, like Hamlet, ill-at-ease. There was so much of which he disapproved: 'There is no denying', wrote Bridges-Adams in *The Lost Leader,* 'that there was in Barker a strain of temperate, fastidious rationalism that rather distrusted the time-honoured apparatus of stage illusion.' In his preface to *King Lear* Barker appears to want Lear to act the storm without thunder. That means by speaking: at least he says nothing of gesture, though asking in an aside, 'What actor in his senses would attempt to act the scene "realistically"?' We learn no more from the discussion of this scene in 'From Henry V to Hamlet' (included in the present volume). There is no reason why the thunder should not be deafening, provided that it is properly orchestrated with the words.

Poetry alone is not enough; the very word 'theatre' means a place for 'seeing'; but to suggest that Barker did not know this is to misunderstand him completely. Shakespearian speaking, with its multiple variations and subtleties, he delineates admirably in his 'Introduction to The Players' Shakespeare'; but it alone never contents him. Illusionary stage effects he rejects. There remains the final key: acting. Here Barker saw vividly what was needed. In writing of this same *King Lear* storm scene in his preface, he observes that Shakespeare had few supporting effects, but:

He has in compensation, the fluidity of movement which the negative background of his stage allows him. For the rest, he has his actors, their acting and the power of their speech. It is not a mere rhetorical power, nor are the characters lifted from the commonplace simply by being given verse to speak instead of conversational prose. All method of expression apart, they are *poetically conceived;* they exist in those dimensions, in that freedom, and are endowed with that peculiar power. They are dramatic poetry incarnate...

The actor has then, not simply or chiefly to speak poetically, but, for the while, somehow to incarnate this poetry in himself.

That is finely said; yet neither it nor what follows is sufficiently
specific to be of practical service.

Acting is Barker's central concern. In *The Exemplary Theatre* (1922)
he looks for a new 'virtuosity' in acting; 'Before ever the literary
man and his manuscript appeared, acting was there, and it remains the
foundation of the whole affair.'

> The better the play, the more full of matter, or the more
> brilliantly evanescent in style, the less excuse has its performance
> for being dull. But the more does it need acting; not only a
> fuller understanding, but a greater virtuosity of interpretation.

In advancing this plea, Barker is even willing to lay aside some of his
most cherished convictions. In 'From Henry V to Hamlet', he says,
'more is involved than the mere staging' of Shakespeare; this is
regarded as subsidiary and not essential. He proceeds:

> But whether it is to be played upon a platform or behind
> footlights, whether with curtains or scenery for a background (and
> scenery which is more than a background sins even against its own
> nature) this at least is clear if my contention of today be allowed:
> Shakespeare's progress in his art involved an ever greater reliance
> upon that other art which is irrevocably wedded to the playwright's
> — the art of interpretative acting.

The nature of that 'interpretative acting' is left to the performer.

'Within my own day', he wrote, 'one school of Shakespearian
acting has perished; it was not a very good one, but it had its own
virtues.' For new advances, conditions are not, he says, propitious.
As an evening's entertainment Shakespeare's 'five great tragedies'
are as unsuitable as a Passion of Bach or a Mass of Beethoven
('From Henry V to Hamlet'). That is, the new 'virtuosity' might not
have public appeal. However, Barker pleads for an attempt.

As an illustration of what might well be called 'virtuosity', I turn
again to Tree — not Tree as a producer, but Tree as an actor. Tree's
well-known recording of Antony's 'O pardon me, thou bleeding piece
of earth' has a quality that might be called 'architectonic'. The
movement is slow and suspended, building up to a climax. The speech

is something made as well as something spoken; it follows Shakespeare's habitual technique in long speeches. I do not expect Barker would have approved, if only on grounds of speed. For Tree as an impersonator, the evidence is before us. We have only to look at any picture of Tree in his various parts: his Malvolio and Othello (reproduced in my *Shakespearian Production*); his King John, in the foyer of Her Majesty's Theatre; or the photographs in Hesketh Pearson's admirable biography *Beerbohm Tree* (1956) and the many more in the important volume of appreciations entitled *Herbert Beerbohm Tree,* edited by Max Beerbohm (undated). In all these you will see not only a mastery of characterisation in make-up and costume, but a use of *the total physique* deployed in significant action which approaches genius: so much is conveyed that you hardly need to see the performance.

If we may judge from an offhand remark in a letter to Gilbert Murray, Barker strongly disliked Tree's acting, though in the introduction to the collected *Prefaces* (1958, Volume 1) he paid tribute to Tree's generosity in inviting Poel to contribute productions to his own Shakespeare Festivals, and in *The Exemplary Theatre* to his 'great public spirit' in founding the Royal Academy of Dramatic Art. Barker deplored in many contemporary actors the lack of all finer articulation of the 'body'. On the incontrovertible evidence of these pictorial impersonations, Tree had exactly this bodily 'articulation'; and his Shakespearian speaking in records of *Richard II* and *Hamlet* — he was particularly happy with such 'artistic' types — as well as that from *Julius Caesar,* is poetically sound, even admirable.

Again and again Barker insists that drama is more than speech. The actor must incarnate, live the poetry. In his 1937 Romanes lecture, 'On Poetry in Drama' (which might have found a place in the present volume), he says:

> Realism or symbolism, verse or prose, rhythm or rhyme — these things and their like finally neither make nor mar. The presentation of character in the person of the actor, that is at the heart of the business, and in the strength or feebleness of that drama lives or dies. Think of a play — as one should — as something which is only complete in performance, and clearly this must be so. The actor is then beyond comparison the most potentially powerful of the forces engaged; and not to employ your best means of expression to its full capacity argues timidity or incompetence in any artist and in any art. No other fictive art has such a vital medium

and all the great dramatists have known how to employ it to the full. But, being vital, it is also unruly; and how to give it scope and not lose hold of it, dominate it without devitalizing it, is a problem not too easy to solve, and – as we said – is the master problem of the acted drama.

The dramatist, we are told, as his art develops, relies less on action and economises 'in every sort of doing so that his characters may be able less disturbedly to *be* what they are'. In *Macbeth* Shakespeare is 'Intent upon showing us and upon emphasizing, not what they do, but what they are'. We are reminded again of Tree's pictures, as close an external impersonation of the character's inner *being* as art could devise.

Barker's extended advice on the actor's art is given in *The Exemplary Theatre*. A high degree of freedom is allowed, since beyond technique the actor has a 'further purpose' in obedience to life, which must not be constricted, even by himself: he should not try to fix a good effect as permanent, or the performance will end up in bits. Performances should be free and allowed to vary. Even improvisation and part-authorship are proposed as future possibilities. It is astonishing to observe how much of this applies to the liberal acting methods of Tree (see Hesketh Pearson's biography throughout; and the conclusion to Shaw's essay in *Herbert Beerbohm Tree*).

So Barker lays down his conditions for fine acting; the rest is left to the performer. It is admirably done; but, for Shakespearian tragedy, I question whether his equipment as an actor experienced mainly in modern plays of subdued tone had the resource for anything more than general advice. He was at an impasse, like Gordon Craig, whose demands on the actor were such that he had to fall back on his *über-marionettes,* though in his *Henry Irving* (1930) Craig does indeed go far to define a great actor's 'virtuosity'. As the Hamlet in our story, Barker killed his Claudius, the old tradition, stone dead; he could then only point to Fortinbras (apt name for our purpose). He was probably wise to retire and turn to writing. For acting, his task was to point the way, and that he has done.

The key to both Craig's and Barker's demands lies in poetic acting; that is, incarnating the poetic *conception* lying within or behind the words by use of the whole body, in big or little ways, moment by moment. It is not today recognised how much lies dormant in this unrespected and unpractised art. Such artistry I have discussed and

defined throughout my *Shakespearian Production* (Faber, 1964;
currently in print as a Routledge paperback), which records my own
attempts to master the acting of Shakespeare's tragic heroes.
(See especially pages 48-58, 165, 236-41, 279-80, 287-88, 312-16.)
Further statements are in the as yet unpublished *Symbol of Man*,
concerned mainly with body-acting.

Such then was the achievement of Granville-Barker: creator of
three exquisite Shakespearian productions in the pastoral vein; author
of commentaries of varying distinction; and prophet of a new
virtuosity in acting. His destruction of a great tradition was needed
and successful; but a new one has not taken its place. Bridges-Adams
did forthright productions under his influence at Stratford. Since then
differences have abounded. Acting has often been impressive.
Production has sometimes been good, given the right occasion. It has
also been appallingly bad. Tree and Barker alike would have been
staggered by the vandalisms that are perpetrated and applauded today.

This article has not been easy to write. Merits and demerits are so
inextricably entangled. An astute critic of my 1948 *Timon of Athens*
at Leeds wrote that I 'achieved the remarkable duality of producing
sensitively in the modern style, but yet acting in the way of the old
school'. Perhaps that may serve to indicate some of the paradoxes that
are involved.

Additional Note, May 1976

I was not myself ever aware of much difference in my acting style
from that of others, but reviews indicate that there has been a
difference. The best account of it occurs in a letter from the dramatic
critic and Shakespearian scholar, Mr Roy Walker, of 12 December
1948, in which, after seeing my 1948 *Timon of Athens* at Leeds, he
says: 'I have never seen anything like your acting, although I have
imagined something like it.' While agreeing with me that it was not
all successful, he proceeded to relate it to the original Shakespearian
tradition and define it in terms of 'gesture, posture, movement,
mind and tongue harmonized into organic life on the imaginative
level of symbolism.' This he regards as 'a glimpse of the theatre
that Shakespeare's poetic texts cry aloud for'. He too observes
a contrast between it and the other performers. I was, I suppose,
instinctively aiming to achieve what I now call 'poetic acting', such as

that for which Granville-Barker seems to have been searching.

A reliable Toronto report said of my Macbeth that I was acting on a 'different plane' from the rest. That is not necessarily to say that I was acting better; since more was involved, I may have been acting worse; but there was a difference. Another Toronto report, arising from a conversation of Raymond and Brownlow Card, similarly regarded it in terms of tradition, mentioning Garrick and Henry Irving. For myself, I have been merely trying, despite a host of inadequacies, to act well; and, if at all possible, to 'get away with it'.

Mr Walker writes to me on 11 May 1976, referring to his opening sentence as follows:

> ...Although I meant it in a wholly favourable sense, I rather meant to stress that your performance was, in my experience, *unique* rather than unsurpassable. That is, I was certain that good acting in Shakespeare's time was a physical poetry as well as spoken poetry and that we'd lost and suppressed it. It must, I was and am sure, have been far more like what your approach led you to do.

Mr Walker is the author of two important Shakespearian studies on *Hamlet* and *Macbeth*: *The Time is out of Joint* (1948) and *The Time is Free,* a richly packed and pregnant work (1949). He subsequently edited the magazine *Theatre,* and wrote dramatic criticism for *The Times.*

For a discussion of stage practice in Shakespeare's time, see B.L. Joseph, *Elizabethan Acting,* 1951.

INDEX